AMERICAN
ANTIQUE
FURNITURE

AMERICAN ANTIQUE FURNITURE

1640–1840

PATRICIA PETRAGLIA

FRIEDMAN/FAIRFAX

PUBLISHERS

A FRIEDMAN/FAIRFAX BOOK

© 1995 by Michael Friedman Publishing Group, Inc.

Library of Congress Cataloging-in-Publication Data

Petraglia, Patricia, date
    American antique furniture: 1640-1840 / Patricia Petraglia.
       p.   cm.
    "Originally published as American antique furniture: styles and
origins"—T.p. verso.
    Includes bibliographical references and index.
    ISBN 1-56799-147-5 (pbk.)
    1. Furniture—United States—Styles.   I. Title.
NK2406.P46   1995
749.213—dc20   94-27973
                                            CIP

Editor: Sharyn Rosart
Art Director: Jeff Batzli
Designer: Paulette Cochet
Photography Editors: Daniella Jo Nilva and Emilya Naymark
Illustrator: Steven Arcella

Originally published as *American Antique Furniture: Styles and Origins*

Typeset by Classic Type, Inc.
Color separation by Scantrans Pte. Ltd.
Printed in China by Leefung-Asco Printers Ltd.

For bulk purchases and special sales, please contact:
Friedman/Fairfax Publishers
Attention: Sales Department
15 West 26th Street
New York, NY 10010
212/685-6610 FAX 212/685-1307

ACKNOWLEDGMENTS

During the arduous task of selecting photographs for this book, I received assistance and cooperation from many museums, dealers, collectors, and auction houses. A special note of thanks to the firm of Israel Sack—while busy compiling pictures for its own publication, it offered valuable counsel and photographs. Gratitude also goes to the many dealers who shared photographs, including Ronald Bourgeault, Leigh Keno, C. L. Prickett, Hirschl & Adler Galleries, and Woldman & Woldman. The combination of photographs represents not only frequently published icons held by public institutions but equally noteworthy examples chosen by dealers, some pieces of which are part of private collections.

Separately, I am indebted to the Michael Friedman Publishing Group for assistance in editing, design, and production. For any errors that may have slipped by the watchful eyes of these professionals, I assume full responsibility.

CONTENTS

INTRODUCTION

Aside from its purely visual appeal as a decorative art, American furniture has a story to tell that reflects the historical events of its various periods. It tells us something about America's past, regarding style and economic prosperity throughout the centuries.

One can draw analogies, for example, between the functional and sturdy component of seventeenth-century furniture and the determined mindset of our forebears. At the same time, the decorative carving on two disparate objects—the sunflower chest of Wethersfield, Connecticut, and the Dennis/Searle chest from Ipswich, Massachusetts—dispels the misconception that early settlers were solely preoccupied with the wilderness and that furniture design lacked creativity.

American furniture of the William and Mary period ushered in the technique of cabinetmaking through the development of the dovetail joint. In its grandeur, a William and Mary high chest not only reflects this development but it became the manifestation of a burgeoning economy, an object of status in the best parlors.

A fully developed Philadelphia hoop-back side chair of the Queen Anne style is an attribute of its period. Beyond the integration of its design based on the S-curve, it represents a sophisticated level of taste and material wealth. In form alone, it has a tangible and sculptural quality that tells us more about eighteenth-century elegance than a two-dimensional painting ever could.

Eighteenth-century Chippendale furniture helps to illustrate crosscurrents in taste and temperament. In Newport, patrons showed an affinity for the serene block-front case of late Baroque form while its sister city, nouveau-riche Philadelphia, expressed a preference for pieces with Rococo carving and a sense of movement. From two Quaker cities came two different presentations, juxtaposing the known with the approaching allure of fashion.

While furniture of the Chippendale era shouted the aspirations of the individuals for whom it was crafted, nineteenth-century furniture of the Neoclassical period, with its quiet, self-assured disposition, whispered affirmation. A positive assertion came from the geometry and grace of Federal forms as well as from the Empire designs that fostered a kinship between the new republic and those of antiquity. The Pillar and Scroll style was the embodiment of a democratic ideal, reflecting America's self-direction in the arts, a by-product of developing technology.

This text was conceived with such a perspective in mind. Period styles are described not only in light of their English and Continental ancestry, but as objects that were the output of a talented and perceptive group of artisans who eschewed certain European forms and decorative dogma in favor of good design with integrity of form and a decorative vocabulary that appealed to the more restrained eye and pocketbook of their American patrons.

The last chapter of this book is devoted to connoisseurship and to the attendant issues of authenticity, repairs, and restoration. Furniture is not immune to the principles of supply and demand that influence commodities in general, and prices continue to escalate as more collectors come to recognize the aesthetic and historical value of a finite universe of American furniture. In economic terms, too many dollars chasing too few goods can spell danger for the uninformed. Some general guidelines are included that have proven helpful to scholars, collectors, dealers, and others devoted to this American decorative art.

Part I ✦ Colonial Furniture
(1640–1790)

Pilgrim Furniture (1640–1690)

William and Mary Furniture (1700–1730)

Queen Anne Furniture (1725–1755)

Chippendale Furniture (1755–1790)

Pilgrim Furniture
(1640–1690)

And who, in time, knows whither we may vent
The treasure of our tongue, to what strange shores
This gaine of our best glory shall be sent
T'inrich unknowing Nations with our stores?
What worlds in th' yet unformed Occident
May come refin'd with th' accents that are ours?

Samuel Daniel, 1599

These words probably echoed in the minds of many eager Pilgrims on the long and grueling voyage to the New World. Many who were lucky enough to survive the trip arrived weakened from the dreadful conditions at sea. The situation once they landed was little better; the first cruel winter claimed more than half the settlers in Plymouth Colony. Perseverance, hard work, and a hefty dose of good luck all combined to carry these remaining brave souls through the first years in a strange land.

The seventeenth-century immigrants to the New World were presented with more challenges than just the physical demands of settling a new location. History books always recount that the Pilgrims set out for the New World to build a society free from the religious and civil injustices prevalent back home. This is accurate, but they also desired to maintain many aspects of their English heritage and material culture. These dual goals influenced the nature of early colonial life in America. Consequently, early cultural life in the colonies differed little from that of many inhabitants' native England.

Although the environment often proved bitter and unforgiving, America was also a land of immense natural resources. These resources, including a supply of timber that had long since disappeared in Europe, motivated those settlers with varying degrees of skill to transform abundant raw materials into objects—furniture, for example—that perpetuated English material culture. These craftsmen ultimately saw their status rise to a level that would have been unheard of in the courts of England or in the capitals of Europe.

With the Great Migration of 1630 to 1640, approximately 20,000 English immigrants found their way to the shores of the regions that became Massachusetts, Rhode Island, and Connecticut. Although some of the new arrivals came from London, many more had their origins in small towns and rural areas. After their initial relocation difficulties had lessened, these individuals joined their previously transplanted counterparts in assembling dwellings and furniture in the styles of their homeland.

By 1670, America was no longer a wilderness outpost. The skilled craftsmen from England and the Continent that were part of the continuing influx to the New World busily erected permanent houses mimicking the construction of the models they had left behind. In New England, these structures were raised primarily from wood. Southern settlers tended to prefer brick dwellings. The typical framed house was built of sturdy oak timbers held together by mortise-and-tenon joinery. And it is here that the history of American furniture making begins.

Style Overview

Courtesy The Henry Francis du Pont Winterthur Museum, DE

Seventeenth-century Pilgrim furniture relied on squared, unyielding, rectilinear forms, like the framework of timber buildings. It was sturdy, useful, and constructed of indigenous woods—mostly oak and pine. Based on its survival rate, much furniture of this period was made in Massachusetts. There are, however, examples from other New England states, including Connecticut, Rhode Island, and New Hampshire. There are also some surviving pieces from the New York area and from the South.

Occasionally, furniture from this period is referred to as American Jacobean, a term derived from the Latin name for James. James I (1603–1625) was the ruling monarch of England when the first settlers set out for America. English furniture has traditionally been named after the monarch under whose reign the style emerged or was popularized.

Using this term to describe colonial furniture of the period is problematic since only a fraction of what constitutes

Pilgrim furniture can claim English Jacobean work as a design source. Much of it, in fact, was an eclectic mingling of Anglo-Flemish Renaissance design elements with a strong Italian influence. In the seventeenth century, these design elements were transmitted to the colonies in a myriad of ways. In order of frequency, they were brought over by craftsmen, by importation of actual objects, and infrequently by pattern books, a sequence that would change in later decades.

Furniture makers of this period were known as joiners and turners. Joiners produced furniture forms that had originated in medieval England. Solid, durable items such as chests, trestle tables, joint stools, and settles were made by quickly piecing together wide boards, often with a mortise-and-tenon joint. In this process, a mortise hole was cut into one piece of wood and a tenon, or tongue, was shaped to fit into the mortise. Another hole might be drilled through the joined parts to hold a peg (or dowel) that firmly secured this joint.

Turners, craftsmen who turned wood on a lathe, made items including seats and bedsteads, much of which has been referred to as "stick" furniture, or pieces constructed entirely from turned members. Turners also supplied the decorative spherical balusters; tapered, split spindles; and bosses or oval "jewels" that acted as surface ornaments on case pieces, including chests.

These bulbous, decorative elements were often painted black to simulate the exotic ebony that might be found on a court-level piece in England. Turned elements provided a much needed contrast to the rigid look of pieces constructed of straight lines joined at ninety-degree angles.

The size and shape of the turned elements—as well as the distinctive nature of any carving—were often the only identifying characteristics of a particular craftsman's work. Continuing research in this area is helping modern scholars to recognize the work of singular artisans or groups of artisans.

Many of these turned elements can be found on Pilgrim furniture after 1660. Furniture spanning this period generally exhibits characteristics that resemble Renaissance-inspired furniture of Anglo-Flemish derivation in form and in surface ornament. The massive cupboard, with its precise proportions, geometric partitioning, and symmet-

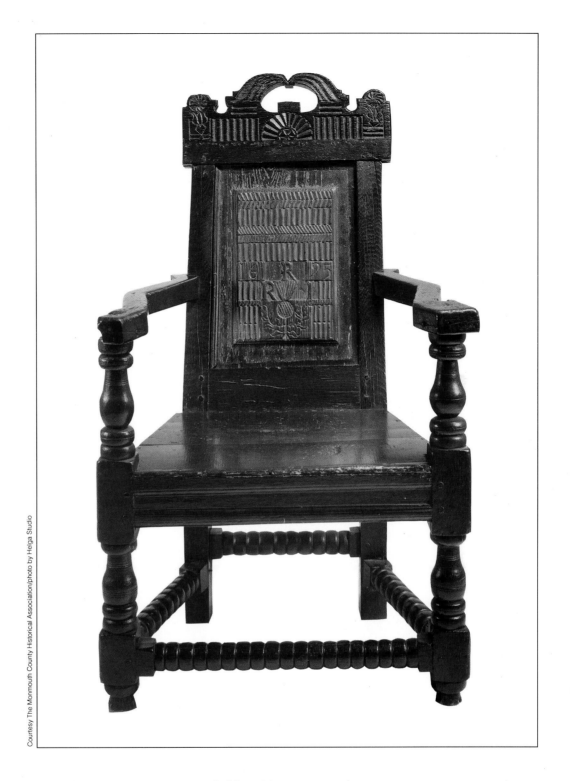

OPPOSITE PAGE: *This massive oak kas with its raised panels reflects the aesthetic preferences of its New York owners of Dutch heritage. From Merrick, Long Island, it is dated between 1650 and 1700.*
RIGHT: *This painted oak with yellow pine wainscot great chair with high back and broad proportions recalls European ceremonial chairs. The carved inscription refers to the owners, Robert Rhea and his wife, Janet Hampton, who married in 1690.*

Courtesy The Monmouth County Historical Association/photo by Helga Studio

rical, repetitive carving, survives as one example of this influence.

Additionally, an adept application of carving and/or paint offered another degree of visual interest. Popular carved motifs included floral patterns: the Tudor rose, the tulip and leaf, and the sunflower. Other, more stylized motifs included one that resembled strapwork, or medieval hammered-iron elements. In all cases, these motifs were fashioned in a relatively flat, two-dimensional manner.

Seventeenth-century furniture retaining its original surface paint is extremely rare. Where it survives, it is an important document of period style, offering an unchanged look at early American material culture. In any case, the examples that follow will help to dispel the misconception that the Pilgrim lifestyle was plain, frumpy, and void of great artistic endeavors.

Case Pieces

"Case" refers to furniture based on the box shape, and intended to hold something. The basic forms were the chest and the cupboard. In the late seventeenth century, the same joiners who were found busily erecting houses could just as easily be called upon to make a chest. By far, the most valued of seventeenth-century chests were "joyned." A chest's rails (horizontal elements) and stiles (vertical elements) comprised the frame; they were grooved to accept the panels they held. Mortise-and-tenon joints held the chest together. These joined chests were the predominant furniture form of the period and held a family's dearest possessions, including textiles, the most prized of all commodities.

One might be lulled into thinking that seventeenth-century furniture was primitive and that a chest produced by one joiner was stylistically akin to any other. But as early as the 1650s, areas of commercial prosperity, differing political boundaries, and religious and regional differences created distinct regions with differences that filtered down to furniture design. Some of these differences are illustrated by the chests of the Connecticut River Valley.

The Wethersfield area around Hartford, Connecticut, is known to have favored a chest with a distinctive tulip and sunflower design. The name Peter Blin (active 1675, d. 1725) has traditionally been associated with this design. Continuing scholarship has suggested that differences in carving and variations in ornament on many of these chests point to other hands at work, thereby suggesting a regional school rather than a single artisan. Some scholars posit that the sunflower is really a stylized marigold, the traditional flower of the Huguenots who arrived on these shores via England.

The Connecticut sunflower chest usually had one or two drawers and stood on four short legs. Partially painted and distinctively decorated, these linear and vertical chests contain clearly defined inset panels of low-relief carving; the carving is contained within the boundaries of the panels. Generally, these chests had three panels of plant motifs. Bosses and spindles, products of the turner's craft, were lathe-turned of softer woods and applied to the chest for additional visual impact. Constructed mostly from oak, these chests are usually dated between 1675 and 1700.

Dated between 1675 and 1700, the sunflower chest from the Wethersfield area of Connecticut showcases joinery, turning, and carving. It is a definitive piece of Pilgrim furniture for the wealth of clues it provides about seventeenth-century taste. **OPPOSITE PAGE, ABOVE:** *Free-flowing carving on this chest from the Hadley region of the Connecticut River Valley meanders over the entire front surface creating a design that relieves the severity of the form. The owner's name, Mary Pease, adds personalization.*

The Hadley chest is named for the Connecticut Valley (Hadley, Massachusetts) area where it appeared in quantity. Its design is frequently attributed to John Allis, Samuel Belding, and their followers.

Structurally, the Hadley chest is akin to the sunflower chest. Oak is the primary wood, and both rely on similar construction techniques. The Hadley chest, usually a chest over one or more drawers, is noticeably taller and more linear.

The sunflower chest had a motif that was used by a closely knit family of craftsmen. So, too, did the Hadley chest. Its motif reflected a design that probably originated in northern England. Application of the ornament, however, points to some major differences between the two types of chest. The Hadley chest's loose carving, representing leaves, vines, and miscellaneous geometric forms, is flatter than the sunflower's. It is not rigidly contained in the panels as is the carving in the sunflower piece; instead, it meanders over the whole front surface.

These details lead to the conclusion that this chest is meant to be seen frontally; the fact that many of the chests lack side panel ornamentation supports this argument. Craftsmen always practiced economy of labor; effort would not be expended where it would not be readily visible.

Unlike the sunflower chest of the Wethersfield area, the Hadley chest displays no applied ornament. Instead, visual excitement was generated with a bright coat of paint. Unfortunately, few of these pieces survive with their original painted surfaces. Many were stripped early in the twentieth century when beginning collectors sought to better pieces by making them appear new. Thankfully, this practice has largely ended.

Imagine, though, the rich contrast that would have existed between the panels on the Hadley chest if they still wore their original red, yellow, or blue-black paint. This ornamentation differs sharply from the applied bosses and spindles found on the sunflower chests. One can be comfortable dating Hadley chests between 1675 and 1720. The Musuem of Fine Arts in Boston is one of many public institutions with examples of both forms.

Closely related to the sunflower and Hadley chests is another type of chest, a carved and painted wonder of seventeenth-century design. When dismantled, this chest is a complex assemblage of carefully notched and fitted pieces. So exact was the fit between parts that each piece was scored with a Roman numeral to ensure the correct sequence of assembly.

Derived from Renaissance concepts of proportion and scale, this cupboard was a luxury reserved for the wealthy.

The large sculptural turnings are characteristic of Newbury, Massachusetts, 1680 to 1700.

Based largely on carving technique, Thomas Dennis (active 1663–1706) and William Searle (active 1634–1667), both working in the Ipswich area of Massachusetts, are alternately cited as the artisan responsible for this style of chest, which is known as a Dennis-Searle type chest. This distinct scrolled surface carving is reminiscent of medieval metal strapwork, and to a degree, helps to soften the hard line of the object's underlying form.

Overall, the pattern recalls a Gothic stained glass window. Once-vivid paint competed with the carving for visual play. Following the lead of other period chests and employing the same economy of labor, this chest, too, was intended to be seen frontally.

Many seventeenth-century households contained these types of chests; however, only the very wealthy could afford a cupboard, which was the most ornate, expensive piece of furniture. For magistrates and ministers, for example, the cupboard was a showpiece of affluence, used to display costly imported ceramics and plates—all material possessions that were beyond the reach of families with lesser means.

Based on period usage, a cupboard housing a cabinet with doors above and an open shelf below was called a court cupboard. A press cupboard had cabinets on top and on bottom.

The chests discussed above parallel medieval form: They are fairly portable, planar, flat, and predominantly horizontal. Decorative elements, especially the strapwork-inspired carving of the Dennis-Searle chest, present this same medieval feeling.

The medieval strapwork-inspired carving on this painted oak chest, circa 1670 to 1700, is the hallmark of Thomas Dennis and William Searle of Ipswich, Massachusetts. The construction is a careful assemblage of notched and *fitted components.* **OPPOSITE PAGE:** *This kas from northern New Jersey is painted in* grisaille, *or tints of gray, to mimic the floral carving on costly European models. Its floral motif reflects the taste of the European Low Countries.*

Seventeenth-century cupboards, on the other hand, are not medieval in style, but show an imaginative blend of Anglo-Flemish Renaissance form and decoration. These massive pieces display Renaissance concepts of proportion and scale, and they are more vertical than horizontal. Further, their swelled size necessitated that they be more permanent fixtures, dispensing with the concept of portability that was characteristic of medieval furniture.

The cupboard still depended on the straight line for its underlying form. Exuberantly turned balusters, spindles, and bosses with a sculptural grounding grew in size to accommodate the piece's grander proportions. They provided a sense of movement, a characteristic that would come to the forefront of furniture design in later centuries. But tastes changed slowly and vestiges of the older, medieval style sometimes remained in the carving.

Again, paint was often used to supply that critical element of visual surprise, setting up contrast between light and dark. Almost intuitively, the craftsmen who built these pieces seemed to understand the fine art concept of *chiaroscuro* as popularized by such masters as Rembrandt and Caravaggio—a dark coat of paint played off against the naturally light colored oak or pine for a dramatic effect.

Imagine the attention these stately objects would have commanded in the late seventeenth-century room. Some might consider them garish and overwhelming by contemporary standards. But it's best to remember that homes were not brightly lit; candles or a roaring fire provided the only source of light.

Seventeenth-century rooms, even in the wealthiest of households, were not bursting with furniture; that concept didn't surface until the Victorian era of the late nineteenth century. One should fight the urge to impose the Victorian idiom of plentiful decorative arrangements onto seventeenth-century interior design.

Even within the small locus of New England, cupboards varied according to the same factors that influenced chest designs. These factors included religious and political differences, the skill level of the particular maker, and his attendant design concept based on regional custom and preference.

While the mostly English settlers in New England preferred the cupboard, the *kas* or *kast,* a large press or wardrobe, appealed to the mostly Dutch inhabitants of New York. The kas was even more vertical and linear than its New England counterpart. It was built of heavy, often raised panels, and was topped with a large overhanging cornice. The total effect of the kas was one of architectural splendor.

The Dutch population was not hampered by some of the sumptuary laws that regulated the Puritan lifestyle of New England. Consequently, in New York pieces there was an abundance of ornament, both inside and out. On the outside, many were painted with the favored Dutch floral motif as a way to simulate the carving that might be found on high-style European equivalents; others had intricately carved and raised inset panels.

The Dutch settlers' interiors might have been enhanced with delft tile, ceramics, paintings, and textiles—all the stylistic preferences of the European Low Countries from which their crafters once hailed. Some pieces of furniture were painted with a monochromatic palette known as *grisaille,* or tints of gray, which was meant to mimic carving.

These beautifully painted kasses qualify as the first still life paintings in America. One example can be found at the Monmouth County Historical Association in Freehold, New Jersey.

In the continuing seventeenth-century tradition, most kasses or presses were built of oak and pine. Like their New England counterparts, they are usually dated from about 1650 into the first decade of the eighteenth century.

Seating

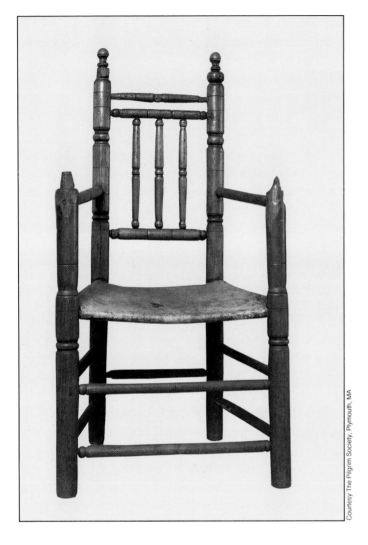

LEFT: *With the exception of the seat, this "stick chair" was fashioned entirely from turned members. A turned chair with spindles on the back only is called a Carver chair.*
RIGHT: *This rectangular chair was derived from the English farthingale or Cromwellian chair that accommodated the full clothing of the period. Elaborately spiralled models were called "twist turned" and were popular in Philadelphia in the 1680s.*

Chairs occupied a unique place in the seventeenth-century interior. Early in the century, if a household had chairs at all, they were reserved for the head of the family, with other family members relegated to stools and benches in typical European tradition. Toward the end of the century, and as family fortunes grew, chairs became more prolific. It wasn't uncommon for a prosperous family to have a set of six, twelve, or eighteen chairs. Such chairs would have been set around the perimeter of a room when not in use and were moved about the room when occasions demanded.

Seventeenth-century chairs also varied in shape and size. The most common variety have come to be known as Brewster and Carver chairs. The Brewster chair, named for a like chair in the possession of Elder William Brewster of the Plymouth Colony, was fashioned of upright turned members with spindles beneath both arms and seat.

Carver chairs, named for one in the home of Governor John Carver of Massachusetts, are closely related to the Brewster chair. Unlike the Brewster chair, though, Carver chairs have turned spindles on the back of the chair only; stretchers (crossbars placed between the legs to strengthen the chair) substitute for the spindles below the seat and arms.

These chairs, dating from the 1620s through the last quarter of the seventeenth century, were made of turned ash, maple, hickory, or elm. Seats were made from boards or plank, rush, or splint. These chairs are also known as "stick chairs." In England, similarly constructed objects were called "thrown(e)" chairs, having been thrown on a lathe. Pilgrim Hall in Plymouth, Massachusetts, has examples of both chair forms.

Degree and quality of ornament found in the turnings are often the only characteristics that separate one artisan from another. A finely executed set of spindles on a Brewster chair, for example, provides a gentle rhythm that contrasts with the chair's linear and vertical stature. Details such as well-turned mushroom finials on the front stiles, sausage-turned armrests, or bobbin finials on rear stiles, are just several decorative features that distinguish a truly great chair of this period from a mediocre example.

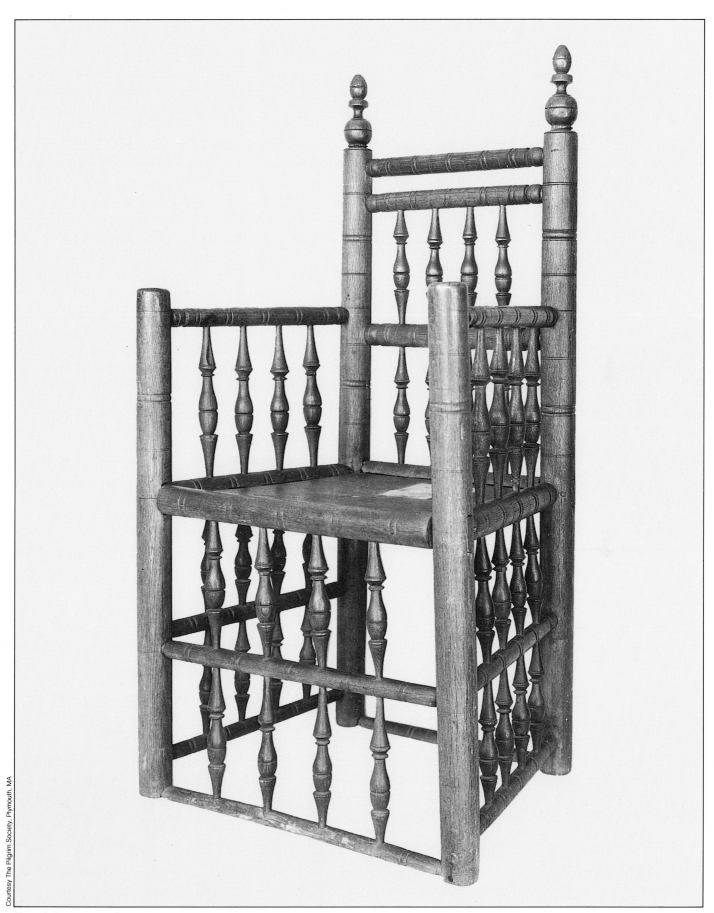

Turned chairs with spindles on the top and beneath the arms and legs are known as Brewster chairs after one in the possession of Elder William Brewster of the Plymouth Colony. This chair can be traced to Governor William Bradford of Massachusetts.

Courtesy The Bowdoin College Museum of Art, Brunswick, ME, gift of Mr. Ephraim Wilder Farley

that was originally found in Russia and Germany. It was brought into Holland where it was shipped to England and to other European countries. The word wainscot was simply a holdover of the term since colonial craftsmen relied on an abundant indigenous supply of oak to build these chairs.

The proportions of the plank seat (which was often adorned with a generous down cushion); the height of the panelled back; and the surface ornaments that consisted of carved dates, initials, and geometric and strapwork details, suggest that these chairs were indeed symbols of authority. Many are suggestive of European religious or ceremonial chairs—and going back even further—ceremonial chairs from antiquity. Consequently, these chairs have almost exclusively been associated with men.

Again the name William Searle (1634–1667) has been associated with the most intricate wainscot armchair of the period. This massive oak chair of squared form was profusely carved with the motifs that have come to be linked with the work of William Searle and Thomas Dennis of Ipswich, Massachusetts, notably S-scrolls and strapwork-influenced carving.

The penultimate tribute to Searle's skill can be seen in the three urn finials that top the piece. They present a crispness and fluidity rarely seen even on the best of English court-level pieces. In conjunction with the chair back, they add more height, a reflection of the owner's status. This chair is dated in the late 1660s, and can be found at the Bowdoin College Art Museum in Brunswick, Maine.

Another chair that typified seventeenth-century design was a chair derived from the English farthingale, an armless chair that easily accepted the full clothing of the period. It is believed that the form found its way to the

The slat-back, or ladder-back chair, was built of four upright posts, with the back connected to horizontal slats. And while the basic four-post construction was the same as on the Brewster and Carver chairs, the overall appearance is slightly more horizontal.

Unlike stick chairs, the slat-back looked more to Dutch prototypes for its inspiration. This is particularly apparent in the characteristically thin and finely shaped slats and in the flange turnings of the finials. Winterthur Museum has a chair fitting this description.

This chair was refined in the eighteenth century, when it exhibited more pronounced turnings, and thinner, higher, and narrower proportions. Eighteenth-century Delaware River Valley chairs born of this earlier type are among the most coveted by today's collectors.

Recalling the form and the decorative elements of many seventeenth-century chests, the imposing oak wainscot chair was a product of the joiner. The term wainscot comes from the Dutch *wagenschot,* or a prime grade of oak panel

ABOVE LEFT: *This seventeenth-century oak wainscot chair from Ipswich, Massachusetts, survives as the finest example of a joined great chair. Its distinctive carving style is the work of William Searle who, along with Thomas Dennis, is known to have favored strapwork-inspired carving.*
RIGHT: *This Dutch-inspired slat or ladder-back chair from New York has a more horizontal emphasis than Carver or Brewster chairs due to the wide slats in the back.*

Courtesy The Henry Francis du Pont Winterthur Museum, DE

colonies from England via Spain and Holland during the brief period (1649–1660) of Puritan domination in England under Oliver Cromwell. It is alternately called a Cromwellian chair.

These rectangular chairs have a clearly defined open space between the back and seat, an opening that was often lessened by a large cushion. Maple, oak, and occasionally, walnut, were the chief woods from which they took shape.

Some were constructed of simply turned pieces. Others were artful examples of elaborately twisted wood that rippled the surface. These heavily spiralled varieties were known by many names in the period, with one of the most popular called "twist turn'd." American versions of these chairs date from the last quarter of the seventeenth century, with the most elaborate ones popular in the 1680s, especially in the Philadelphia area. Some were expanded horizontally into couch form.

Additionally, most Cromwellian chairs had one feature that distinguished them easily from their peers—fixed upholstery. Upholstery served a multiplicity of purposes. Not only did it provide comfort against the wood, but it increased the visual appeal of a decoratively simple form. Its appearance marked the start of concern for comfort in furniture design.

Boston was the center of manufacture for thousands of these chairs that were consumed locally as well as exported to other English colonies. They were often sold in sets; probate inventories from the period allude to sets of six, twelve, and eighteen.

Leather, one type of upholstery, was stretched tautly over a filling of grass or wool pile. Brass nails following the outline of the chair accentuated the chair's verticality and height. Often referred to as "rose-headed" (for the shape of the four tapered sides), these brass nails were entirely forged by hand until the late eighteenth century.

An even more distinctive covering consisted of brilliantly colored knotted pile fabric. Called "turkey work," this upholstery was woven to simulate Middle Eastern tex-

This maple and oak couch from Boston still retains its original turkey-work upholstery. The geometric knotted pile fabric was made in England to simulate Middle Eastern textiles and is a rare example.

tiles. The colorful geometric fabric was woven in England and was used to cover these chairs as well as to make cushions, bed hangings, or to adorn a table.

Because the fabric was less durable than leather, chairs with an original turkey work surface are extremely rare. So precious was this jewel-like turkey work that it was often passed on as a family heirloom. The Essex Institute in Salem, Massachusetts, has a couch with its original turkey work upholstery.

The settle, or wooden bench, was shaped from pine, maple, and less frequently, oak and walnut boards that were solid to the floor. This box-like structure had a high, solid back and arms, and occasionally a wooden hood. Its form resulted in a foundation that provided for hidden storage, sometimes a hinged seat over the lower box.

The settle, by nature of its enclosed back, helped to ward off the drafts that afflicted seventeenth-century houses. Period usage found most settles placed before the hearth. The larger models could also serve as a less formal room divider. Settles with numerous shared characteristics were made from the end of the seventeenth century to the middle of the nineteenth century, making dating diffi-

cult for all but the most experienced of scholars.

Rounding out seventeenth-century seating furniture was the simple joint stool and the "form." The joint stool, sturdily constructed of oak or pine planks resting on simple turned legs, was an indispensable object. Quite portable and used mostly by women and children in accordance with medieval custom, the stool did double duty: Used foremost as a seat, it could also be pressed into service as a table.

A "form," derived from medieval prototypes, was simply a horizontally extended joint stool. Many stood on outwardly splayed legs that added an extra measure of strength and balance. Forms were used with long, joined trestle tables. The very act of seating two or three people on a form was a social event. The painting, *The Peasant Wedding,* by Peter Breughel the Elder was painted a century earlier and depicts a European event but it demonstrates perfectly the many ways that these pieces were put to use.

The increased production of individual chairs in the next century marked the demise of the form and the joint stool as standard seating pieces. The scarcity of these pieces today is indicative of the hard life they saw.

Besides the main objective of providing seating, large settles such as this walnut with leather model could also serve as an informal room divider.
OPPOSITE PAGE: *The product of pragmatic design and simple joinery, this walnut table from the South could be easily taken apart when not in use. It was ideally suited to smaller households.*

Tables ✑

It is widely recognized that a room in the average seventeenth-century home was multifunctional; it wasn't uncommon for families with ten members to all be engaged in different activities in the same room at the same time. Privacy was an unheard of notion. As far back as 1631, Thomas Dudley, huddled by the fire amidst his entire family, commented "...they break good manners, and make mee many times forget what I would say, and say what I would not."

Consequently, knockdown tables, like some trestle tables, used simple joinery and pragmatic design to accommodate this pattern of living. These pieces could be easily taken apart by lifting off the tabletop board or slab and by removing those members that held the frame in place.

An example at Colonial Williamsburg illustrates their simple yet practical form. These pieces, as well as the tilt-top table with its top that pivoted up, could then be easily stored against a wall.

Folding tables, dating from the last half of the seventeenth century, ranged from those with one simple leg to as complex as a table with twelve legs. These tables are generally classified as gate-leg if the leg has a stretcher. Lacking a stretcher, other tables of this group are called swing leg (more popular in the eighteenth century). In terms of decorative ornament, some of the best examples of this type would hold their own vis-à-vis the court or press cupboard. A luxury version with finely turned balusters or spindles could be found draped with a crisp white linen cloth or with turkey work.

Bedsteads ～

What in today's terminology is referred to as a bed, in seventeenth-century terminology would have referred only to the soft goods, or the mattress and its stuffing. Bedsteads, or frames, from the period survive with less frequency than many other pieces of furniture. Early probate inventories, however, suggest a diversity in their number that matches other period pieces.

The most simply constructed and ornamented bed was a joined bed with a panelled headboard reminiscent of early dower chests. Models that were low, set on wheels, and meant to be stored under a larger bed were called trundle beds.

Turned bedsteads that are similar in form and in decorative turnings to those found on the Brewster/Carver stick chairs were alternatives to the heavy, joined bedstead. Lighter in scale, the best examples had spindles that set up an interesting mix of solid and void.

The most expensive bed in terms of its ornament was the "French bed" after French court models. Designed to be swathed in a plethora of textiles that included valances, curtains, and bases, this bedstead was usually lighter and simpler in construction than the joined and turned frames. Bedsteads dressed in this manner would, by virtue of the expensive textiles alone, compete with the cupboard as the object of status in an upscale household.

Courtesy The Pilgrim Society, Plymouth, MA

OPPOSITE PAGE: *According to tradition, this Dutch (or possibly Boston) wicker and leather cradle, circa 1620, held Peregrine White, the first child born in Plymouth Colony.* RIGHT: *The same attention to detail that was invested in furniture meant for adult use was lavished on this joined and turned cradle from Plymouth, Massachusetts, circa 1660 to 1690.* BELOW: *A low, panelled, joined frame typifies the trundle bed. Models on wheels were intended to be stored under a larger bed during the day.*

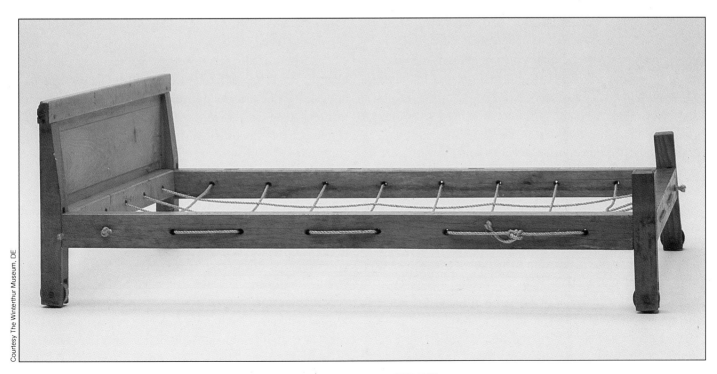

William and Mary Furniture
(1700–1730)

There is no Fashion in London but in three or four Months is to be seen in Boston.

English visitor to Boston, 1700

At the turn of the century, increased trade with London stimulated interest in English and European style and fashion. The skilled craftsmen who had emigrated from England and the Continent interpreted and executed these changing styles. The first decades of the early eighteenth century saw meteoric growth in colonial fortunes with the emergence of prosperous merchant and land-owning classes. These changes had implications for eighteenth-century material culture.

In a significant departure from land-holding traditions in England and Europe, virtually all settlers in America received land from which they could extract a livelihood. Of course, those settlers who had been at the top of the social heirarchy back in England received larger grants than their fellow immigrants who had held lower social status. This allowed them to maintain prestigious enclaves in the colonies following in this matter, at least, the practices of their forefathers. Early colonial life also followed tradition in that it was entirely based on a farming economy. Nevertheless, major differences existed to distinguish colonial lifestyles from those in England. For example, early eighteenth-century colonial life was more permanent. In England, the landed classes moved from season to season, as local resources were used up. In the colonies, the so-called landed gentry provided capital for economic expansion. While still maintaining the basic elements of a land-based economy, these families used their profits to develop and invest in mercantile endeavors that were destined to bring them immense wealth. Mutual economic interest usurped heritage and religion as the bond that united different economic groups. The cities of Boston, Newport, and New York, founded in the first wave of immigration, were joined by new urban centers such as

Philadelphia (founded 1682) and Charleston (founded 1670), towns that sprang from the wilderness to become local hubs of culture and trade. By this time, colonists had settled most of the Atlantic seaboard from northern New England to Virginia and the subtropical clime of the Carolinas.

Historians note that the more firmly rooted and enterprising families dominated their communities economically and politically, establishing power-bases that were unique mixes of the feudal manor and the "corporate" heirarchy. The tentacles of mercantilism had begun to sink into the colonial mindset.

Groups of merchants networked with each other, providing access to the diverse markets of London, Boston, Virginia, and the West Indies. The influence they wielded eventually exceeded that previously exercised by the clergy. Many of the trading networks, like those patterned after the English and Dutch East India Trading Companies, operated under a laissez-faire policy, outside of government mandate. This trade scenario was so favorable to colonial merchants that the English Board of Trade understandably called for reforms to protect its sphere of influence.

In the colonies, social rules became more structured; the individual grew sensitized to his or her surroundings. People became cognizant, for example, that their homes and furnishings reflected their social status. By this time, homes of any significance counted among their contents porcelains, textiles, and silver. Houses that were constructed early in the 1700s assumed a symmetrical and orderly design, a natural outgrowth of the admiration for logical thinking that characterized the period. Even in the early days of the eighteenth century nothing happened in a vacuum. Furniture changed accordingly.

Courtesy Israel Sack, Inc., NYC

ABOVE: *Attributed to John Gaines of Portsmouth, New Hampshire, or Ipswich, Massachusetts, this Flemish chair represents its period well with its slender, vertical proportions, cane, carving, and paintbrush feet.*

OPPOSITE PAGE: *The bureau-cabinet combined drawers for storage and a writing surface in a single unit. This model from Flushing, New York, is resplendent in its thin, meandering floral motif of Dutch origin.*

William III of Orange, ruler of Holland, and his English wife, Mary Stuart, moved from the Dutch to the English throne in 1689 after the Glorious Revolution of 1688. They brought with them Dutch and Huguenot craftsmen who would be instrumental in establishing a forum for changes in furniture styles.

Furniture popular during the period approximating 1700 to 1730 is, by way of simplification, referred to as in the William and Mary style. But just as incongruous as it was to refer to all Pilgrim era furniture as Jacobean, so too is it an oversimplification to refer to all furniture of this period as William and Mary.

It is true that William and Mary played a role in a major style shift early in the eighteenth century. But radical changes had already transpired in England before William and Mary ascended the throne. These changes were the fertilizer that nourished a bountiful crop of new decorative ideas.

In the 1660s—after the overthrow of Cromwell's Puritan protectorate—Charles II had returned from exile in France and Holland. Charles, along with his wife, Catherine of Braganza (whose dowry was the largest in Europe), brought in competent artisans who introduced a wave of new styles in furniture and crafts.

Portugal, Catherine's native home, and Holland were at the epicenter of world trade at that time with far-flung overseas empires. Decorative arts from those countries therefore integrated influences from all parts of the globe. Oriental elements, for example, began to appear in Continental furniture after the trading companies introduced pieces from the Far East to the home markets. New forms and designs emerged, then, not only out of the Anglo-Dutch union of William and Mary, but out of the Anglo-Portuguese marriage of Charles and Catherine.

William and Mary furniture exhibits typical Baroque stylistic undertones. Baroque style was a European design movement that stressed drama and exaggeration in form and in decorative embellishment, a natural outgrowth of late Renaissance style.

In Italy, it was fully developed by 1620; France borrowed and classicized it under the watchful eye of Louis XIV. It ultimately surfaced in England and became an indirect influence on the colonial William and Mary style (and, later, Queen Anne style) in the early 1700s.

The appearance of the William and Mary style in the colonies is thought by historians to have signalled a symbolic shift of power from the once-powerful Puritan oligarchy to members of the merchant class, who maintained strong ties to England. In the mid-1680s, a Royal Governor was installed in the colonies, possibly facilitating this shift.

During this period, colonial furniture retained the flat, rectilinear forms of the earlier Pilgrim style, especially on large surfaces. However, pieces began to incorporate restrained movement and vertical emphasis. This movement served to soften the overriding masculine attributes of the earlier style.

A William and Mary tall chest, or highboy, for example, would still be crafted from a box-like structure or cabinet but it would stand on an exuberantly turned base that was interrupted by shaped stretchers.

Following in this movement toward exaggeration, chairs grew in height and were adorned with painstakingly carved scrolls. Carving became almost sculptural in its effect. Many chairs had caned seats and curved "spoon" backs, a direct influence from the Orient.

As the turner's skill level progressed, so did the decorative turnings. They became robust and divergent. One could take the shape of a trumpet or vase; another might resemble a bulbous bun. Serpentine, X-shaped stretchers gyrated and pulsed, intensifying the sense of movement.

Walnut became the wood of choice in the William and Mary period. It was easily carved and its beautiful grain could be polished to a lustrous finish. Natural variations in color, combined with permutations obtained from cutting either burls or roots, produced a surface that dazzled the eye. Substituting for walnut were maple and pine; it also was common practice to use these less dear woods as secondary components in case pieces. Secondary woods are not usually visible when a piece is fully assembled. Many secondary woods, therefore, were chosen for their economic and structural benefits, and not necessarily for their aesthetic appeal.

The technique of veneering, a labor-intensive method of cutting, fitting, and gluing thin decorative strips or sheets of wood onto a solid surface or carcass, became a common method of increasing the decorative effect of a piece. Inlaid strips of contrasting grains often outlined the veneered strips.

Japanning was another popular system of surface ornamentation. Japanning simulated Oriental lacquer; the term actually applies to the Western interpretation of the Oriental technique. The process, which dates from Eastern antiquity, reached Europe in the 1600s and North American shores, in a modified version, in the early 1700s. Oriental lacquerwork is the art of coating the surface wood with varnishes that are then dried in heated chambers. Figural, animal, and floral motifs on the surface were built up with gesso (a mix of chalk, whiting, glue, and water that acts as a primer) and were then partially gilded or silvered.

Prior to the 1700s, decorative brasses (furniture hardware such as drawer handles) on colonial furniture were scarce. William and Mary furniture made ample use of imported decorative brasses from England. These brasses were crafted into drawer pulls and escutcheon plates (metal plates that backed drawer pulls or surrounded keyholes) that reflected candlelight off their effulgent surfaces.

All of these changes in underlying form, construction technique, turnings, surface carving, and ornament required a specialized set of skills. As a result, the William and Mary phase saw a greater division of labor; objects were no longer the exclusive domain of a single artisan.

Among the colonists there were no formal guilds corresponding to those of Europe; instead the colonists favored an apprenticeship system. Many localities operating under the mandate of mercantilism and acting for the betterment of the community established regulations governing trade. Apprenticeships in Boston and New York, for example, were set at four and seven years, respectively.

In a diluted version of the European guilds, specific craftsworkers became associated with particular skills: Turners shaped legs, stretchers, and balls; carvers supplied the ornamental C-scroll crests. The upholsterer began to play an increasingly important role both as a purveyor of fabric and interpreter of taste.

But the biggest change centered around the assembly process. The task of assembly was now entrusted to the accomplished hands of a cabinetmaker. Unlike massive case pieces of the past that were held together with mortise-and-tenon joints, the thinner and more attenuated William and Mary pieces called for a new system of joinery.

Cabinetmakers—as distinguished from simple joiners—abandoned the mortise-and-tenon joint that had served joiners well since the Middle Ages. Instead, cabinetmakers opted for the more sophisticated dovetail joint, or a method of joining boards at the ends with interlocking tenons in the form of a dove's tail.

Sophisticated style centers were able to duplicate a high-quality joint. Separate pegs were no longer necessary. Those cabinetmakers with developing skills initially turned out mediocre versions, perhaps a drawer with one large crude joint, until practice allowed them to refine their work.

The American William and Mary style, an outgrowth of European Baroque design elements tinged with Oriental influences, formed a bridge between the Medieval/Renaissance-inspired furniture of the Pilgrim era and the modern styles of the eighteenth century. The William and Mary period ushered in cabinetmaking techniques that persist today.

Case Pieces ∽

Coastal Connecticut pieces still favored the tulip and vine motif while eastern Massachusetts chests rendered with paint pictured foliage and architectural buildings. Some of these chests were nicknamed "Harvard chests" due to their similarity to the brick buildings at Harvard, even though a factual connection has never been made. It is more likely that the architectural motif was a holdover from that found on English nonesuch chests that once depicted Henry VII's Nonesuch Castle.

As for motifs, much of this decorative painting mimicked japanning, although its extreme flatness is more readily aligned with *trompe l'oeil* painting than with true japanning and lacquerwork. All details, for example, lack

LEFT: *Unlike earlier chests where paint was used primarily as a solid backdrop, William and Mary chests employed paint in a representational manner depicting motifs that were once carved. Based on exotic birds, trees, and leaves, this chest is attributed to Robert Crosman of Taunton, Massachusetts.*

By the beginning of the eighteenth century, furniture makers were no longer the same professionals who built houses. A continual influx of craftsmen had created a wealth of skilled labor in the colonies. These artisans in turn produced the latest fashions, including the coveted high chest, the item that supplanted the stately cupboard as a household object of status.

The main construction technique relied on the dovetail joint, and eliminated the process of butting heavy oak sides to even weightier frames. The lighter dovetail technique allowed the cabinetmaker to frame drawers and chests of thinly sawed pine; materials were used more judiciously.

Chests with multiple drawers—the William and Mary version of the dower chest—appeared as another result of dovetail construction, which permitted the stacking of lightweight drawers. The chest of drawers now had a higher center of gravity.

Chests from eastern Massachusetts and coastal Connecticut were essentially squared boxes whose severity was relieved by swelled bun feet. Decorative ornament consisted of paint delicately applied as a basecoat and then covered with a contrasting motif.

the gesso undercoat that gives depth to authentic japanned work. Instead, these details are painted close to the surface and lack the artistic profundity of Oriental examples.

Imported drawer pulls in the quintessential tear-drop shape finalized the decorative ornament. These pieces, dating from about 1700 to 1725, remain as pleasing examples of a provincial or vernacular aesthetic, balancing masculine form with delicate painting.

Pennsylvania turned out some of the most stylistically advanced chests of drawers. One type, a squared walnut case with graduated drawers, accentuated its form with bold moldings and squat bun feet. A gracefully slender and symmetrical light-colored vine and berry inlay danced across the front surface of the drawers. Dated primarily around 1720, the decorative inlay is occasionally found on pieces from the mid-eighteenth century.

The high chest of drawers, or highboy, as it would later come to be known, had a top geometric section or case of drawers that stood on a base of Baroque-inspired turned legs connected by stretchers. These pieces were not without problems: The large case section stood on a fragile base that sacrificed sturdiness for aesthetic appeal.

OPPOSITE PAGE: *Coastal Connecticut chests with multiple drawers favored the tulip and vine motif. This chest from Saybrook, Connecticut, dated 1726, is essentially a square box whose angularity was relieved by swelled ball feet and teardrop drawer pulls.*
RIGHT: *Dated 1724, this painted chest from coastal Connecticut has a thin carcass made possible by dovetail construction, a turning point in furniture design of the William and Mary era.*

A high chest with a carcass of maple and maple-and-walnut curled veneer typified the New England version. Moving from top to bottom, most began with an architectural cornice, thick or thin, and progressed down the square form to drawers graduating from small to large. Molding outlined the drawers, preventing them from being visually lost within the richly patterned and veneered surface.

Additional arched molding was applied where the top case met its base or frame. Made in two pieces for ease of movement, many high chests have seen extensive repairs or replacement, especially to their bases. Early models from around 1700 had a single horizontal drawer as part of the base while highboys dating from 1720 onward often contained multiple drawers in the base.

Bases ended with arched skirts that rested on ornately turned legs of inverted cup, vase, or trumpet form. These arches were a visual transition point from the horizontal orientation of the chest top to the vertical uplift of the turned legs. It was customary to affix thin beading to arches in a manner that followed their curves.

On the best examples of this form, stretchers, connected to the legs, followed the curve of the skirt, further unifying the design. Like the turnings they connected, stretchers were a vulnerable design point but provided a fractional measure of support for the legs. Small bun feet connected these horizontal stretchers to the floor. The surface of the New England high chest was the most dramatic of its elements. The highly figured maple-and-walnut veneers applied to the facade made a seemingly static top come alive with depth and movement, a movement that was interrupted only by strategic placement of conservative tear-drop brasses and lock plates.

The veneer process was well suited to flat surfaces; turned legs were painted to simulate the veneered case or were ebonized. The veneered surface was a practical response to the rich surface treatments that made up the decorative lexicon of European Baroque design.

Patterns that resembled seaweed or tortoiseshell recall *boullework,* named for André-Charles Boulle (1642–1732), the French cabinetmaker, or *ébéniste,* who worked under the patronage of Louis XIV. Boullework introduced the inlay of brass, pewter, ivory, and mother-of-pearl to wood or tortoiseshell, creating masterpieces whose beauty transcend time.

By contrast, the New York high chest, like an inscribed one at Winterthur Museum in Winterthur, Delaware, presents a geometric format. It is wider, rigidly con-

ABOVE: *The high chest replaced the cupboard as the status object in the William and Mary period and beyond. This example from Flushing, New York, is unusual because it was signed by its maker, Samuel Clement. A New York model had a relatively plain surface* compared to New England versions whose surfaces were highly figured. **OPPOSITE PAGE:** *A rare example of early eighteenth-century case furniture, this walnut bureau-cabinet from Philadelphia is stamped "Edward Evans 1707."*

structed, and highlighted by straight bands of lighter-colored inlay that define the graduated drawers. The eye does not penetrate the surface as it does in a New England chest.

The New York chest relies instead on the inherent qualities of the polished red gum and ash to play off against bright drawer pulls and escutcheons. Brasses play a more important role on this chest as they are not competing with heavily figured surfaces. Legs and feet on New York examples are generally more flared and sharp-edged than those of New England chests. Stretchers follow the arches of the skirt.

The eighteenth-century dressing table, or lowboy in modern terminology, was a short profile case of drawers that stood on turned legs. Many were turned out en suite with the high chest, resulting in a balanced, coordinated arrangement that made a powerful statement of status. Frequently topped with a mirrored device and outfitted for holding toiletries and jewelry, the dressing table became an invaluable grooming aide.

The bureau-cabinet was a multifunctional unit. The structure housed drawers for storage and a writing surface, or what the French referred to as a bureau. The bureau-cabinet paved the way for the freestanding desk with drawers, a refinement of the cruder slant-top writing boxes of decades past. Most bureau-cabinets date around the first decade of the eighteenth century.

A Philadelphia bureau-cabinet of black walnut with pine, now in the collection of Colonial Williamsburg, stands as an enduring example of sophisticated urban craftsmanship. Signed and dated "Edward Evans 1707," it is an extremely rare document; signed pieces in American furniture, especially before mid-eighteenth century, do not frequently exist.

Since there were no closely formed guilds similar to those in Europe to control production, a maker's stamp or signature was not standard fare. Many pieces that were once believed to be signed by a maker are actually carved with the name of the owner, a practice that can make attribution difficult, especially when dealing with as-yet-unidentified artisans.

The Evans example follows the structure of the high chest. And like the high chest, the bureau-cabinet progresses down from a molded cornice and mid-section molding. Instead of standing on turned legs, however, the top box rests on another box-like drawer configuration that sits on slightly compressed bun feet.

The front facade of the top section falls forward to produce the bureau, or writing surface. Behind the writing surface is a row of slots or pigeonholes followed by a series of smaller drawers. A larger center storage compartment flanks these inside drawers and often housed the important documents of the growing merchant class.

Surfaces were simple, relying on proportion, brasses, and a walnut veneer that possessed a gentle brilliance from layers of imported shellac or varnish.

A bureau-cabinet made in New York about the same time, and now at Museum of the City of New York, is a fraternal twin to the Pennsylvania cabinet's form, scale, and construction. But unlike the quiet surface of the Penn-

sylvania bureau-cabinet, the facade of the New York bureau-cabinet is awash with highly stylized floral sprays, always the favored Dutch motif.

Whatever one's decorative preference, these chests, with their graceful proportions, work on all levels, from the intricate floral inlay on the New York piece, to the richly figured and polished walnut on the Pennsylvania piece. Both are important documents of regional preferences and point to the heightened skill level of the maker.

The William and Mary period saw the writing part of the desk integrated with its base for the first time. This furniture form was called a chest of drawers with desk. Probably derived from the French *escritoire*, or writing desk with drawers and pigeonholes, in this country, they were mistakenly called scriptors, a bastardization of the French term.

Virginia favored cabinets with drop lids on open stands that were imported from Boston. A regional school of Boston cabinetmakers endorsed one inlay pattern in particular—a curly and meandering eight-pointed star, otherwise referred to as a compass inlay.

Seating ❧

During the William and Mary era, individual chairs appeared with increased frequency. Following Baroque design imperatives, they became leaner and taller than their seventeenth-century counterparts. What a William and Mary chair gave up in bulk, it made up for in height: On average, a William and Mary chair surpassed its predecessor by eight to ten inches (20 to 25 cm).

Stylistically, chairs showed distinction between the colonies, but the majority drew inspiration from English examples. Within the colonies, chairs marked the biggest group of imported furniture—quite a change from the previous decade, when most people still used backless stools for seating.

Boston was the center of production for thousands of caned chairs that were pieced together with near assembly line virtuosity. The slender, vertical proportions, turned members, and carving reflected the Baroque influence at its strongest.

Organization was consistent from one chair to another. These chairs had turned front and rear stiles or vertical members of sinewy and block form, and turned horizontal stretchers, caned seats and caned insets in the back separate from the rails. Tall backs usually terminated in carved crest rails that repeated the pattern in the bottom rail, and most were styled out of maple that had been painted black.

Nowhere was the Baroque language stronger than in the carved motifs. One of the most popular of these was the Flemish scroll in which the lower curve, a C-scroll, is separated from the upper scroll, a reverse C-scroll, by an angle that measured roughly ninety degrees.

Daniel Morot, the French Huguenot architect and designer—and a Boulle protégé—followed William and Mary to England. He is often cited as the father of this richly detailed and fluid carving style.

Caning, the application of woven split strips of Asian rattan, reflected the growing trade with the Orient. It also reflected the Anglo-colonial penchant for exotica: Cane, lacquer or japanning, porcelains, and tea were all popular manifestations of this fad.

The front legs of the cane or Flemish scroll chair concluded with the Spanish foot, although the foot's true ori-

Courtesy Shelburne Museum, Shelburne, VT/photo by Ken Burris

ABOVE: *The banister-back chair was a more economical version of the Flemish scroll chair with costly cane or leather backs.* **OPPOSITE PAGE, LEFT:** *The Boston chair, as it was known in the period, was the ubiquitous William and Mary seating* piece. **OPPOSITE, RIGHT:** *A gate-leg table stands in the center of the room and banister-back chairs are placed against the wall when not in use, a habit that followed period practice. The wool window treatments are rare eighteenth-century examples.*

gin was Portuguese. This gently sloped and ribbed foot has a forward curling bottom and is alternately known as the "paintbrush" foot for the ribs that resemble the bristles of a brush.

While it is often difficult to distinguish colonial cane chairs from their English precedents due to stylistic similarities, the colonial versions tend to be simpler. The best cane chairs of this period married Baroque and Oriental influences in a chair that was graceful, a pleasing contrast of solid and void, and a tribute to the art of the carver.

The Flemish scroll or cane chair was at the ornamental end of the decorative spectrum. By contrast, the Boston chair (its period name) was simpler. This tall leather upholstered chair of painted wood was normally devoid of carving. The back was fashioned from plain stiles; even the crest rail was more modest. Boston's Museum of Fine Arts is just one of many institutions that counts the form in its collection.

Turned legs ended in Spanish, double ball, or scroll feet. Like the void on cane chairs, the space between the stiles was partially filled in with a back. Models built toward the end of the period began to carry a rounded or spoon-back of Chinese derivation anticipating the Queen Anne style.

The Boston chair became the ubiquitous William and Mary seating piece and was shipped throughout the colonies. When compared to the Flemish model, the Boston chair has less interplay between solid and void; it has a heightened sense of stability. Since the squared form and embellishments changed little from chair to chair, turned members on the front stiles and stretchers allowed for some degree of differentiation.

Painted maple frames (and the rare bare wood frame) had leather upholstered backs, and seats followed in the footsteps of earlier Cromwellian chairs, but their taller proportions and Spanish feet clearly point to Baroque composition. Double rows of brass-headed nails held down the leather and were the only applied ornament. A testament to its popularity, this chair was produced well into mid-century and was the linchpin of Boston's furniture trade.

Other regions also propagated the successful style, creating an intercolony rivalry. One advertisement in the *Pennsylvania Gazette* claimed: "Made and to be sold by Plunket Fleeson...black and red leather Chairs, finished cheaper than any...imported from Boston."

The beginning of the eighteenth century saw furniture making grow from a cottage industry to part of the larger mercantile economy in the cities of Boston, Newport, New York, and Philadelphia. But changes filtered into rural areas as well. Rural New England, like provincial England, reproduced European styles in underlying forms but continued to simplify urban embellishment or decoration.

Courtesy The Museum of Fine Arts, Boston, MA, gift of Mr & Mrs Dudley Leavitt Pickman

Armchairs were called "elbow chairs" in the eighteenth century. Slightly idiosyncratic in its design, this chair from coastal New England pairs sculptural elements on the crest and hand supports with the five upright banisters.

The banister-back chair best demonstrates this provincial tradition. The banister-back chair had a back made from vertical turned banisters or balusters, finished on top with a cross rail and on bottom with a matching turned stretcher. The narrow spindles are suggestive of balusters that were used in staircases of the period, and served to link the decorative arts to architecture.

Banister-back chairs have backs that are as vertical as the backs of Delaware River ladder-back chairs are horizontal. New York and the Delaware River Valley continued to prize the horizontally focused ladder-back that was

introduced at the close of the last century and that was simultaneously being refined.

The banister-back side and "elbow" or armchair showed Baroque makeup: tall proportions, turned four-member construction from maple, scrolled carving (often of flatter projectile), and crested tops. They also flaunted distinctly provincial idiosyncracies of interpretation and execution. The coastlines of New Hampshire, Massachusetts, Connecticut, and New York served as the centers of manufacture.

Economical versions used thrifty rush in place of imported cane for seats. With the exception of the banister components, these chairs followed the structural skeleton of other William and Mary chairs. The most discriminate feature was the carving of the chair's crest. Many scholars place great emphasis on this singular feature when assigning date and regional attributions.

The Stratford, Connecticut, area turned out a banister-back chair that was called a heart and crown chair after the motif on the crest rail. The shop of Thomas Salmon (1693–1749) is one of several credited with this motif.

Pennsylvania banister-back chairs represent different stylistic tendencies, including the output of yet-to-be-named craftsmen. Compared to Boston models, Pennsylvania chairs assumed a quiet elegance. Less fussy than many Boston types of high-style London heritage, these chairs used a simpler rounded crest rail that followed provincial English design dictates.

Compared to Boston's graduated and flowing crest rails, Pennsylvania's use of the simple rounded crest is conservative. Such a conservative approach was offset by artistically turned stiles that reflect a comfort and experience in the craft.

Another chair of ebonized maple, circa 1710–1730, portends the coming Queen Anne style in its stylized splat, sculptural silhouette, and crest rail. The turned frame is in the spirit of other banister-backs with the exception of its one wide and flat vase-shaped splat in the chair back. This contrasts with the multiple vertical members of the other banister-backs.

Ram's head handrests and Spanish feet added another level of sweeping drama. Chairs of this type were the hallmark of John Gaines III (1704–1743) of Portsmouth, New Hampshire.

Corner chairs or roundabouts were an invention of the William and Mary period. Their development complemented the desk. They were the preferred seating at desks, hence the alternate name, writing chairs.

Other than the stool, the corner chair is the shortest of the William and Mary seating inventory. Structurally, it has one leg in front, one in back, and one at each side. The back is a horizontal rail that has been bent or rounded to accommodate the sitter's back; the back is on two sides. Corner chairs from the early 1700s had no splats between the seat and back rail. The later addition of wide splats was an invention that acquiesced to comfort.

Due to the rising acceptance of individual chairs with integrated backs, stools did not appear in the William and Mary era with as great a frequency as in previous years. Those that were made might be upholstered with flame-stitch embroidery, called *bargello* or Hungarian work. Settles lingered on from the previous decade and remained little changed.

The daybed or armless lounge chair was designed for repose during the day. Similar to a chaise lounge, the daybed had a back that was canted or tilted. The seat and back rest were of "Cain," or "India," type, or less frequently, upholstered.

A New England example of walnut and maple was an ornate relative to its English equivalent. Carved crowns and scrolls, foliage, and bulbous blocked and turned legs were standard fare in New England. The southern colonies favored the sturdier mortise-and-tenon construction and less carving, resulting in a plainer surface.

Standing on six to eight multi-turned legs and stretchers, these low slung couches created interesting geometric patterns that surpassed sixty inches (1.5 m) in length.

The upholstered easy chair arrived in North America at the end of the seventeenth century. However, it wasn't until the William and Mary period, with its emphasis on comfort and luxury, that the form flourished. Padded maple and pine frame chairs had "wings" that stopped drafts, and were overstuffed and covered with a wide range of fabrics.

Contrary to contemporary usage, period inventories suggest that easy chairs were usually located in the bedroom where those of ill health or of advanced age could enjoy the chair's warmth and security. As far back as the 1590s, an ailing Philip II of Spain sought comfort in a chair of this type.

Since the plain-twilled or fancy-patterned wool that covered these chairs was imported, clues to regional identity were found in the turned bases and seat and crest profiles, as well as in the shape of arms and wings.

These easy chairs occupy a position of historical importance that far outweighs their ability to keep a sitter warm and comfortable. This chair forever changed the furniture

Made between 1720 and 1730, this walnut daybed from Charleston, South Carolina, was intended for repose during the day. Even though the top of the crest is missing, a degree of restrained movement is still evident in the back.

trade; never before had the skills of the upholsterer been so significant. For the first time, it was this vocation, more than that of the turner, that set the pace of interior design—an influence that continues today.

The upholsterer was the eighteenth-century equivalent of the interior designer. Along with providing the uphol-stery for the easy chair, the upholsterer selected bedding, window treatments, and other textile elements for the home. Upholsterers became the consummate purveyors and arbiters of style. And along with the century-spanning easy chair that initially elevated their status, they continue to flourish.

The appearance of the upholstered easy chair with its high back and wings heralded the beginning of concern for comfort in furniture design. The elderly and infirm sought their comfort in the bed chamber.

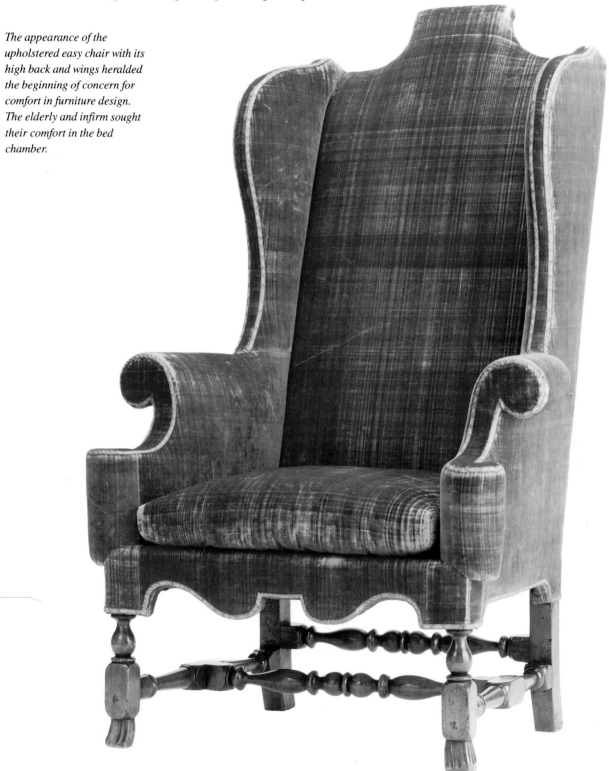

Tables ∾

The specialization of tables that began at the close of the seventeenth century continued through the William and Mary period thanks to the increased buying power of the colonist. The new tables were classified according to the function they served: dressing tables, side tables, and candlestands.

Folding or gate-leg tables increased in number throughout the first quarter of the eighteenth century. Length of leaves dictated the number of supporting gates. A single gate-leg or tuck-away had a small top that swung down when the gate was closed. It was favored in homes of limited size from Massachusetts to much of the South.

Though not exclusively a colonial invention, the butterfly table, a gate-leg table named for the moveable wing-shaped brackets that support the leaves, is closely associated with Connecticut. The Wadsworth Atheneum in Hartford possesses a handsome example. Achieving a more graceful outline than traditional gate-legs, the butterfly table stands on outward-slanted turned legs that in their more advanced design break the cube-like confines of earlier models.

Details that help crystalize regional traits on tables include baluster and cup turnings in New York; butterfly supports in New England; cup and trumpet turnings separated by reels and noticeable spaces between drawers in Pennsylvania; and unevenly sized adjacent drawers in the South and in Pennsylvania.

ABOVE LEFT: *This burl maple and walnut-veneered dressing table from south-eastern Massachusetts is a rare document of a table with its original finish. The stylized inlaid motif on the top as well as skillfully turned trumpet and vase legs show the maker's attention to detail.* **LEFT:** *A gate-leg table with superbly turned legs and stretchers. Period usage would dictate that it be draped with a crisp white linen cloth or with turkey work. When closed, this table was a space saver.*

Queen Anne Furniture

(1725–1755)

An imaginary gentleman "talks all day long of frieze, cornice, and architrave, [and] there is not a gate-post near his house nor a broomstick in it which he has not had... carved according to some one of the five orders."

The Universal Spectator, 1730

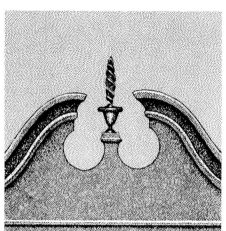

The economic expansion that began several decades earlier continued through the 1720s in both Britain and America. In the commodity-driven colonial economy, wealth was created by those with an astute mercantile sense. Grain, lumber, and molasses comprised the base of their trade. Even the human element was commodified, with the slave trade pitting Newport against Boston for the prosperous Caribbean routes.

At about this time, England abolished cumbersome import duties on North American timber. Black walnut, or "Virginia" walnut, as it was known in England, found its way into English cabinetwork.

Patterns of increased trade—as well as Queen Anne's War—drew colonial America steadily into international affairs. This war, staged on the soil of New England, Carolina, and the West Indies, became the New World equivalent of the War of Spanish Succession. After it ended in 1713, peaceful growth characterized the era.

Inter-colony trade grew. *The Vade Mecum for America: Or a Companion for Traders and Travellers* cited highways and points of interest from the boundaries of Maine to Virginia. Trade between the coastal cities of New York and Charleston grew to such a degree as to prompt scheduled postal delivery service by 1728.

As geographic mobility was extended so, too, were intellectual pursuits. Increased ease of travel, a greater component of leisure time, and the economic prosperity that an ever-widening mercantile economy afforded led the colonists to value education and knowledge. Where in the previous century they needed all their wits for mere survival, now the colonists sought intellectual stimulation.

One requirement of a good education was a thorough grounding in the study of architecture, the most important components of which were respect for classical orders and respect for proportion. Imported architectural books—believed to number more than eighty-seven different titles in colonial America—were largely responsible for the transmission of design ideas.

Needless to say, these principles dictated building design. Built in 1737, Thomas Hancock's Beacon Hill home reigned, until its destruction a century ago, as one of New England's most impressive dwellings. Its Georgian plan was most certainly derived from English architectural manuals.

A broken-scroll pediment topped the building's balcony window, the stone of which was fashioned in Middletown, Connecticut. This fact alone may account for the similarly shaped but provincially executed pediments found on doorways throughout the Connecticut River Valley.

Many of the most ambitious colonial residences were built during this period. John Drayton, a member of the king's council, built Drayton Hall outside of Charleston on the banks of the Ashley River. William Byrd II presided over the construction of his country home on the James River in Virginia. James Logan, William Penn's secretary, built Stenton outside of Philadelphia.

In 1740, the first edition of *The City and Country Builder's and Workman's Treasury of Designs* appeared. Along with housewrights and others engaged in the building trade, cabinetmakers sought guidance from the principles outlined in its pages.

At one end of the architectural-cabinetmaking spectrum sits the Speaker's Chair from the House of Burgesses at Williamsburg. Its monumental proportions, panelled sides, and triangular pediment make it all but indistinguishable from architecture.

Conversely, provincial furniture from New England made by those less conversant with architectural mandates loosely adapted such architectural features and only hints at this connection. Overall, though, in the course of American design, Queen Anne furniture complements the architecture of its period.

Style Overview ✍

Art historians have suggested that when an artist explores a particular visual aesthetic very explicitly over approximately thirty years, aesthetic priorities then shift so that successors follow a different course. The same might be said about the decorative arts, with particular reference to the transition from the William and Mary style to the Queen Anne style. By the late 1720s the exaggerated, heavy C-scrolls and bulbous turnings of masculine character gave way to the refined, graceful, and sublime curvature of the Queen Anne era.

What has come to be known as the Queen Anne style had little, if anything, to do with the personage of Queen Anne, who ruled England from 1702 until her death in 1714. In fact, the term was coined much later, in the nineteenth century, by antiquarians seeking a descriptive label for the distinctive curve of the furniture that was dominant in America in the second quarter of the eighteenth century.

This method breaks somewhat with earlier English tradition, in which a style is named for the ruler who supported and popularized it. By the early eighteenth century, nomenclature no longer necessarily followed royalty in England.

The English Queen Anne style marked a stylistic departure from European trends to a greater degree than did earlier English fashions. In the early eighteenth century, England felt outside influences less, and much of its furniture became stylistically domesticated until mid-century.

Due to the time it took for fashions to reach the colonies, the so-called Queen Anne style didn't appear there until about 1730, long after the death of Anne. It is therefore more accurate to describe colonial Queen Anne furniture as a style that incorporates characteristics from several periods, especially those traits that have been linked to Georgian design.

Traditionally, late colonial stylistic developments are not described as Georgian, although Georgian styles were certainly a part of colonial life, both in architecture and in furniture design. Contemporary scholarly efforts have recently acknowledged this influence to a greater degree. The close link between American and English design traditions cannot be disputed; but perhaps those patriotic nineteenth-century historians one century closer to the Revolutionary experience chose to avoid paying homage to anything Georgian. In any case, the Queen Anne label helps to crystalize an aesthetic in vogue from 1725 to 1755, and in some instances, even longer.

It was during these years that culturally refined colonists developed an interest in architecture. So avid was this interest and so eager was the architectural amateur to display knowledge in this area that, according to Horace Walpole, one woman had "a petticoat decorated with columns of the five orders."

In many ways, pieces from the Queen Anne period reflect a unity of design that surpassed anything that preceded or followed them. There are several reasons why this is so. One of the most compelling factors was the architectural underpinning that guided furniture design. Another contributing factor was the overwhelming focus on a predominant design component: the S-curve.

In England, cabinetmakers had rediscovered the influence of Italian Renaissance architect Andrea Palladio (1508 to 1580) through his English disciple, Inigo Jones (1575 to 1652). The revival of British Palladian style in the 1720s was largely due to the work of William Kent (1684 to 1748), who published *The Designs of Inigo Jones* in 1727.

Kent was the first British architect to design furniture for his buildings. The Neo-Palladian buildings emphasized classical balance and grandeur of scale; Kent wanted the interiors to enhance this new style. The furniture that graced the interiors of these houses used many architectural features and was decorated with large-scale figurative sculpture. It tended to be massive, to reflect the grandeur of the exterior.

These ideas quickly found their way across the Atlantic, where they gained momentum in the colonies, and were modified to suit a less grandiose colonial taste, especially in the Federal period.

Large case pieces were adorned with bonnets that repeated the flowing curves of architectural pediments. Furniture, like architecture, broke free from the geometric constraints of linear construction, and for the first time in the colonies, reached a symbiosis with its surroundings.

On a more detailed level, Queen Anne furniture was more than a careful assemblage of its parts. Historically, furniture prior to this point tends to be dissected and viewed according to the quality of its various parts, by the shape of a leg, by the nature of its carving, or by the choice of materials.

Well-executed Queen Anne furniture, however, derives its strength and beauty from the interaction of its parts. It isn't a style about transition points or great contrasts of thick and thin. The all pervasive S-curve is largely responsible for this unity. The S-curve emerged to become the primary shape of this period, and it reached its pinnacle in the cabriole leg. Formed with an outward curved knee and a tapered, inward curved ankle, the cabriole leg brought much-needed variety to an eye that had exhausted itself on the square or turned legs of the past.

The cabriole was a more realistic leg, one derived from forms found in nature. Whether introduced secondarily courtesy of the *pied de biche,* or doe's foot popular on late Baroque and Régence French furniture; the Italian *capriola,* or hind leg; or the Dragon's foot holding a jewel, brought from the Far East by Dutch explorers, the primary source of the cabriole shape can be traced back to antiquity.

The English painter, William Hogarth (1697–1764), described the S-shape as the "line of beauty." His drawings of cabriole legs with differing degrees of curve inspired cabinetmakers; legs assumed the cabriole shape and pieces took on a three-dimensional quality.

The curve of the cabriole leg was echoed everywhere in furniture, from the skirts on case pieces and tables to the scrolled pediments on high chests to the silhouettes of chairs. Early Baroque juxtaposition gave way to late Baroque orchestration. If the William and Mary style signified restrained movement, then the Queen Anne style signified continuing movement.

The idea of a unified design was further reinforced because objects were no longer viewed exclusively from the front. Their undulating lines and surface treatment were often carried through to the side.

Carving was used judiciously, but in its selective placement and level of technical excellence, it remained an enduring quality. Most often limited to the knees on legs, to the crest rail, and on case pieces, to the crowning finials or arches of the skirt, it served to outline what was already an inherently graceful composition.

Motifs included the stylized scallop and the acanthus leaf. Veneering continued to be applied to drawer fronts and to chair splats, becoming slightly less popular toward the end of the period once the dawn of Rococo design made it less practical—veneering and inlay are procedures that work best on straight surfaces.

Decorative inlay eased a bit as well, although the star or compass inlay stood out as one prevalent pattern. The occasional application of gilding, or gold powder, was used sparingly, always with the intention of punctuating rather than agitating.

Japanning, the surface ornamentation that was popular in William and Mary furniture, made the transition to Queen Anne furniture, although colonial japanning techniques were simpler than European processes that more closely adhered to Oriental format.

Boston continued to be the center of japanning work in the colonies. In the japanning process, the surface—usually of maple and pine—was coated with several layers of vermillion streaked with lampblack to create a tortoiseshell effect.

The japanner laid out the design, raising some of the design with a build up of gesso coated with gold. Next, certain details were painted on the tortoise surface with gold; raised gold portions received more lampblack. Final layers of varnish provided the lacquer effect.

Due to the fragile built-up nature of japanning, and due to changes in humidity that cause these pieces to crack and flake, few japanned pieces survive without some degree of restoration. Indeed, only about thirty-three japanned objects from the eighteenth century survive; many similarly decorated objects were japanned at a later date, probably in the nineteenth century.

Three of the most prolific Boston japanners were Robert Davis, William Randle, and Thomas Johnston, the last of whom is believed to have japanned the most celebrated of all pieces from Boston. This piece, a high chest called the Pimm highboy and now residing at the Winterthur Museum, is named for the chalk inscription "Pimm" on its drawers.

John Pimm was the cabinetmaker responsible for the chest, which is dated 1740 to 1750. Thomas Johnston (also spelled Johnson) was born and trained in England and was active in the city of Boston between the years of 1732 and 1766.

*Known as the Pimm high chest for the inscription of its maker,
John Pimm, this japanned high chest from Boston is the consummate
example of the Queen Anne aesthetic.*

Although comfortable with this attribution, scholars have been unable to conclusively document Johnston as the japanner for the Pimm chest. In any case, the architectural pediment, overall S-curve design, and japanned surface married the disparate elements of Classicism and Orientalism, creating at once a consummate example of excellence and a pragmatic alternative to costly European technique.

In the choice of materials, walnut was still by far the favored wood, with chestnut, maple, pine, and cherry following. Santo Domingo mahogany, available for the first time as the result of growing international trade, steadily grew in use, especially by Newport and Philadelphia cabinetmakers.

The introduction of the Queen Anne style in the colonies coincided with intensifying regional preferences and expressed a heightened degree of sophistication and luxury. Conservative New England held on to incidental William and Mary features, at least initially. Stretchers connecting chair legs, for example, were no longer a structural necessity, yet they could be found on many chairs from the region.

Massachusetts preferred tall, lean pieces and notably slender cabriole legs. Rhythmically composed but simple, chairs from New England were less ornate than their Philadelphia counterparts. Boston was the undisputed urban center of New England during the seventeenth and early eighteenth centuries. But as early as the 1740s, its economy began a slight decline. Newport, Rhode Island, on the other hand, began its climb to commercial prosperity, becoming the center for original design in the Queen Anne period well through the 1790s.

Initially, Newport's Quaker craftsmen created a version of Boston Queen Anne high chests and tables with uniquely pointed pad feet. Later, this close-knit group of artisans, notably the related Goddard and Townsend families, who practiced their craft with success through the nineteenth century, conceptualized and implemented one of the most decorative contributions of the period.

They introduced the Continental concept of blocking and carried it to a height unheard of even in Europe. The process of blocking, or forming raised and depressed areas from solid pieces of wood, was a labor-intensive technique that demanded a sophisticated cabinetmaking acumen. Blocking rose to become one of the most important decorative contributions of the period in Newport, Boston, and in the regions that operated under the stylistic influence of these areas.

While the furniture industry in New York City matched that of Newport in this late colonial period, its great wave of growth did not occur until after the Revolution. Comparisons between New York and Newport, however, prove invaluable in pinpointing the effects of coastal trade on style; craftsmen moved with coastal trade patterns. Certain Newport and New York high chests, for example, have the shared feature of removable legs for ease in shipping.

Newport produced some of the best crafted and most original of the Queen Anne designs. New York City, its population largely comprised of Loyalists, dutifully followed English precedents in furniture design, both in form and ornament.

Philadelphia continued its robust growth, with Philadelphia chairs of the 1740s and 1750s marking the summit

OPPOSITE PAGE: *With its broken scroll pediment and mathematically proportioned case, this high chest shows some of the same concern for architecture as did the interiors in which it was placed.*
RIGHT: *Several features mark this 1739 high chest by Ebenezer Hartshern as typically New England, including the highly figured surface, the flat-top arches of the skirt, and the carved shells. The star inlay was favored in the Boston area.*

of late Baroque chairmaking. Such chairs today are coveted by collectors everywhere.

Furniture from the middle colonies of New Jersey and Maryland often followed Philadelphia practice, while furniture from the South, like that of New York, revealed still-strong ties to English prototypes, whether of high-style or provincial origin. Walnut, fruitwood, and yellow pine provide clues to southern origins, and combined with less tall and stouter proportions, differentiate southern pieces from those of New England.

In this period, colonial skill and taste reached their highest level. And in accord with the equilibrium reached between the surface and its ornament, Lord Shaftesbury professed: "In short, we are to carry this remembrance still along with us that the fewer the objects are besides those which are absolutely necessary in a piece, the easier it is for the eye by one simple act, and in one view, to comprehend the sum or whole."

Case Pieces ✑

Courtesy Shelburne Museum, Shelburne, VT/photo by Ken Burris

metamorphosis. What emerged was a high chest that showed respect for architectural proportion and for the precise line of the S-curve.

Certain characteristics that carry a New England construction discipline include, to name several, five-section upper cases, four-drawer lower cases, flat-top arches in the skirt, and a carved shell drawer in flat-top chests. Chests with pediments may also contain an additional shell in the upper case.

A walnut and pine high chest inscribed with the name of its maker, Ebenezer Hartshern, and the date, 1739, epitomizes high-style Massachusetts taste. Composed of solid walnut sides and pine drawers with matched walnut-veneered fronts, the chest exudes warmth and a sense of movement.

LEFT: *Known as a flat-top high chest due to its straight cornice and flattened arches in the skirt, this model is from the Upper Connecticut River Valley area of Norwich.* **BELOW:** *Curly maple provides the exuberantly figured grain on this Queen Anne slant-top desk from the North Shore of Massachusetts.* **OPPOSITE**

PAGE: *In form and ornament, this japanned high chest from the Windsor area of Connecticut, circa 1736, is an idiosyncratic version of high-style Boston chests. Its "springy" cabriole legs end in hockey-puck feet and its flat but whimsical painting is remindful of* trompe l'oeil *painting.*

Courtesy Israel Sack, Inc., NYC

E arly in the Queen Anne period, the high chest was more stylistically similar to its forebear, the William and Mary high chest, than not. Known as the flat-top due to its straight cornice and flattened arches in the skirt, this type of chest exchanged the multiple turned legs of the William and Mary model for four cabriole legs.

The result was a chest that blended the developed characteristics of the William and Mary period with emerging elements from the Queen Anne style. Most of these date around the second quarter of the eighteenth century.

As the Queen Anne aesthetic and its attendant architectural slant took hold, the flat-top high chest underwent a

Architectural ingredients include the broken pediment or bonnet with its harmoniously executed halves that repeat the S-curve of the cabriole legs and replaced the pilasters on the front of the top case. The pilasters, or flattened columns, help contain the figured surface and complement the piece's architectural orientation.

Ornament is confined to bat wing brasses, two subtle inlays, and gilt shells. One inlay helps to define the drawers. The other inlay is a star configuration that is repeated in several spots. The most visually captivating pieces of ornament are the carved and gilded shells on the upper drawer and on the bottom of the case.

Gilded finials in an open flame pattern somewhat uncharacteristic of New England add a further dimension of verticality by carrying the eye upward. They serve another purpose as well: These finials, in addition to the small pendant drops on the skirt, carry the eye past the geometric confines of the case. The small pendants are symbolic vestiges of the multiple legs they replace.

Standing ninety inches (225 cm) high on slender cabriole legs that terminate in pad feet, this high chest powerfully showcases the New England penchant for tall, slender proportions.

This statuesque chest sets up a delicate balance between the surface and its ornament, and through the many hands involved in its production, testifies to a highly task-specific labor pool. That each craftsman involved understood the total design mandate is obvious; the piece is more than the sum of its parts.

Some of the finest furniture made in southern New England came from Newport. The fact that Newport artisans signed or labelled much of their work has aided scholarship immensely in identifying work characteristic of their region.

Early flat-top models were constructed of walnut with chestnut and pine, but it was the richly figured Santo Domingo mahogany that ultimately came to typify most Newport furniture.

ABOVE: *This desk and bookcase from Boston is the earliest example of dated block-front furniture. It is signed and dated "Job Coit Jr/ 1738."* **OPPOSITE PAGE:**

Cherry was the wood from which many Connecticut high chests were made. This bonnet-top high chest with carved center drawers retains some original drawer pulls.

A flat-top high chest by Christopher Townsend, part of the Goddard-Townsend cabinetmaking dynasty, was notable for such distinct features as squared cabriole legs with narrow knee brackets ending in fine, pointed slipper feet.

The legs are separate components that attach to the case, a feature common in Newport pieces that were destined to be shipped. The skirt is enhanced with gently undulating curves of such fluidity that they reach a crescendo in one center drop pendant.

At the tail end of the Queen Anne period, Newport high chests adopted the scrolled cornice and some other features that came to be known as typically Newport. One was the claw-and-ball foot with undercut talon. Another, the shell-and-volute pattern, might have been introduced to New England by Job Townsend.

Extremely fine dovetailing is yet another hallmark of the Goddard-Townsend shops. This form, along with masterfully executed blocked pieces, was characteristic of the Newport school of cabinetmaking to the end of the eighteenth century.

Philadelphia and the Delaware River Valley pieces in general followed the squared form of New England case pieces but are often differentiated by the trifid foot of Irish derivation. This panelled foot with three sections resembles toes covered with a sock. A high curved skirt with a curved cut-out drop substitutes for the more classical pendant drop on New England versions. Scale is different; Delaware River Valley pieces are raised on thicker legs that create an increased sense of stability.

Blocking was a process new to American furniture-making in the Queen Anne period that reached its zenith in the Chippendale years. This labor and skill-intensive process involved cutting raised blocks of wood from the solid surface.

Since in almost every case the panels were sculpted or cut from the facade and not applied, only the very accomplished cabinetmaker would dare to attempt it. Economy of labor yielded economy of material, especially when working with costly Santo Domingo mahogany. With only a few exceptions, New England furniture crafters in general made judicious use of woods when constructing the carcass.

Blocking was practiced exclusively in New England and most successfully in Newport and Boston. Once transmitted by Continental craftsmen, the blocking design became so firmly entrenched and domesticated in the colonies—especially in the city of Newport—that it endured for a long time after European taste would have labelled it passé.

In most applications, the block-front technique divides the facade into three panels: the center concave, the two flanking sections convex. In the capable hands of a skilled cabinetmaker, a blocked panel would be primarily flat, curving gently at the edges. In profile, the blocked section would break geometric confinement to provide a flirtatious sense of movement.

Those less proficient in the technique turned out blocked pieces that lack design integration; indeed, the blocking appears applied and causes the eye to pause rather than to glide over the surface as it does on well-turned-out examples.

The desk with bookcase was the most accomplished of Queen Anne designs and carried considerable prestige.

Many Boston examples were outfitted with a system of pigeonholes, shelves, and drawers.

Models from the 1740s and 1750s had door panels with arched tops; later models included serpentine edges around these panels. Glass was often fitted into the panels in imitation of high-style English examples.

One example at the Winterthur Museum, originally belonging to the Hancock family of Boston, remains the earliest example of dated American block-front furniture. Made from black walnut and pine and standing an imposing ninety-nine and one-half inches (249 cm), it is signed and dated, "Job Coit Jr/1738." Coit is the earliest cabinetmaker associated with blocking.

The beauty of the walnut is interrupted only by some brass pulls and escutcheon plates; one spiralled finial sits atop a plinth that divides the quietly scrolled pediment.

The New England dressing table was another vehicle that favored the block-front ornament as it progressed from the table into a full blown case piece. An early Queen Anne dressing table often had a slab top resting over one long drawer over an arched skirt. It stood on cabriole legs.

The dressing table gradually progressed to a case with stacked drawers and a slab top defined with thumbnail molding, or molding that in profile resembled a thumb. Such molding smoothed sharp edges and helped create the now prized overall design unity. An arched or scalloped skirt completed the layout. These small details characterize the essence of Queen Anne style and illustrate the period's distinctive concern for design cohesion.

On New England versions, a regional characteristic is a top that sits directly on the case. Examples from Pennsylvania often feature a molded lip between the slab top and the case. Pennsylvania tables of this form often have wider spaces between the drawers and trifid feet.

Charleston carvers incorporated fleur-de-lis and shells with their cabriole legs. This served to reinforce the visual link of the leg with its case. Southern colonies frequently produced versions with less graceful cabriole legs; some were more bowed than curved. The most refined and the dearest of tables had tops that traced the shape of the curve of a skirt or, in bird's eye view, the projections of the block-front design. Tables from New England adhered to this principle most successfully.

Unlike those from the geographically contained major style centers of Boston, New York, and to a lesser degree, Philadelphia, pieces from the widespread towns of the Connecticut River Valley show the influence of various stylistic currents that reached there circuitously. Connecticut pieces thus experiment with the vocabulary of the late Baroque Queen Anne style in a way that differs from those objects that were the output of a cohesive regional school.

This has lead to the oft-quoted phrase: "If it's odd and cherry, then it's from Connecticut." And while they share certain similarities in form and in ornament with furniture from high-style centers, Connecticut pieces have idiosyncrasies that reveal wonderful personalities of their own.

A Connecticut high chest, for example, might have a flat top; thick, springy cabriole legs; and turned hockey puck feet. Decorative paint might substitute for the veneered surface of a more expensive model. A step top was another option that facilitated the display of ceramics.

Seating

pad or Dutch feet, often connected by obsolete turned and joined stretchers. A slip seat fit into the frame and was easily removable for ease in upholstering.

While the Anglo-Chinese chair incorporated certain rudiments of late Baroque style in its construction, the hoop-shaped chair enveloped it and carried it to a level of refinement not even seen on many standard English models.

LEFT: *The front cabriole leg and solid, wide-back splats place this corner or roundabout chair in the Queen Anne style. The seat is a slip seat.* **BELOW:** *With its tall, upholstered back and seat, the slipper chair was used in the bed chamber, possibly by women of small stature.* **OPPOSITE PAGE:** *These fully developed walnut Queen Anne chairs from Newport have a mellow old patina, a sculptural essence, and Georgian-inspired traits that include the hoop-shaped crests and wide compass seats. The voids between the splats and side stiles form the Newport-associated feature of a sharp-beaked bird of prey.*

No item of furniture better epitomized Queen Anne style than the chair. Gone was the rectilinear frame; cabriole legs, horseshoe seats, curved splats, and rounded stiles captured the essence of Hogarth's precise line or S-curve.

Queen Anne chairs demanded much of their makers. The challenge was to balance beauty of design with physical comfort and durability. Chairmakers met this challenge and turned out products that were the embodiment of mid-eighteenth-century elegance.

The transition from the preceding William and Mary style was not instantaneous; elements of the waning style were sometimes mixed with new forms. Conservative New England craftsmen employed this strategy frequently. Chairmakers, for example, often retained the stretcher connecting the legs even though it was no longer structurally necessary.

Queen Anne chairs universally followed one of two forms. The first type was of Anglo-Chinese derivation and was a natural stylistic progression from the Boston chair.

Tall and lean, this side chair had rather straight stiles, a spoon-back that accommodated the spine, and a flat crest gently curved at the ends. It stood on cabriole legs with

Characterized by wider, hoop-shaped crests, often with carved ornament; wide compass, or horseshoe slip seats, and cabriole legs, the Georgian-inspired chair had an inherent sculptural quality. The compass seat, with its very rounded front curve, sometimes continuing into a horseshoe shape, got its name from the process that used a compass to scribe the lines of the seat frame. Today, this seat is often referred to as a balloon seat.

Pad feet or claw-and-ball feet were often at the discretion of the consumer; claw-and-ball feet do not necessarily signify a later date as many antiquarians once believed. They were simply a more expensive option.

Differences in these chairs highlight regional practices at work. Templates were commonly used and the unique nature of the patterns they laid out are a major component in determining the hand of a particular artisan and/or his cabinetmaking shop.

When assembled, the voids or open spaces between the splats and side stiles that these templates helped set up provide clues for regional attribution. Many of the patterns mimic birds' heads.

Massachusetts chairs depict round-headed birds with short bills. On a Newport chair, this space is more sharply outlined, resulting in an alarming bird of prey head with a sharp beak. Philadelphia chairs fall somewhere in between, leaning slightly toward the Newport head but sporting a softer bill.

In examining chairs from two regions—New England and Philadelphia—differences in regional construction techniques become apparent. Specifically, a Rhode Island chair has squared rear legs connected by stretchers to the front legs. Its front cabriole legs end in claw-and-ball feet, and in Newport, the claws are undercut and crisp.

Seats were upholstered with a variety of fabrics. Wool

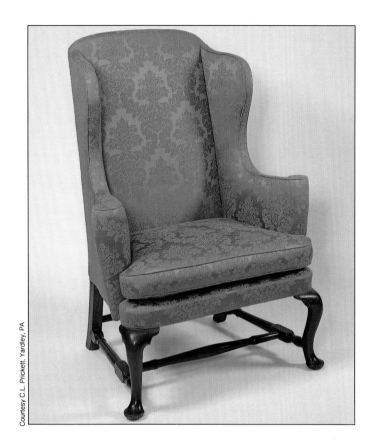

was one of the most widely accepted covers, and several treatments resulted in a broad range of pattern availability. Zigzag or floral patterns known as moreen were created by pressing the fabric with a hot plate.

Normally devoid of carving, for decorative effect the chair relied upon the grain and warmth of the walnut, the twist of the cabriole leg, and the interesting patterns of splats that set up a contrast between solid and void.

A Connecticut chair of this type is recognized by its extremely thin splat and occasional use of the *cyma* curve on the front seat rail. Cyma, from the Greek for wave, represents the double curve. Other Connecticut clues include the choice of cherry, a wood in abundant supply in the area, and a trapezoidal seat with square corners. The overall interpretation is slightly rigid.

Chairs from the Portsmouth, New Hampshire, area display a more eccentric and provincial handling of the form. The synergy between solid and void is disturbed, resulting in a chair that tends toward the willowy.

Newport, like neighboring Boston, most often used the dated stretchers of flat or block form and gently curved thin splats. Occasionally, the cabriole leg had a C-curve on the knee and a front rail that was deeply cut.

The Hudson Valley turned out a chair that was a combination of turned elements that recalled the William and Mary style and the more up-to-date cabriole leg. Its most current feature was the vase-shaped splat.

Philadelphia produced a simple walnut side chair of quiet presence that might have appealed to the Quakers, but the city is best remembered for a second, more decorative form of Queen Anne chair. It is Georgian in derivation, especially in its generous proportions. Philadelphia chairs of this type marked the apotheosis of Queen Anne grace and fashion.

A Philadelphia chair of this dressier English form has no stretchers; the rear legs are rounded stumps or chamfered. Front cabriole legs end in the drake or trifid foot or in the more sturdy and flattened claw-and-ball.

Seat joinery differs, too. Seat frames on Newport chairs are typically mortised-and-tenoned together, with one pin supporting the seat. The Philadelphia chair also has its seat frame mortised-and-tenoned to the rear stiles but the tenon is visible or exposed in rear view. Two pins support the seat. Some Connecticut chairs share the visible through-tenon, a method several Connecticut cabinet-makers picked up while training or apprenticing in Pennsylvania.

In Rhode Island, makers made the seat rim an integral part of the frame. The front cabriole leg is fastened at the corner of the seat frame, with the leg pegged through tenons that are mortised-and-tenoned into the leg. Squared, vertical glue blocks add another degree of strength.

There are differences in surface ornament. Knee carving on the Newport chair is in the form of a stylized scroll with C-curves or a shell with pendant. Naturalistic shells or boldly carved acanthus leaves or "grasses" grace the Philadelphia knee.

Carved details for crests showed two interpretations of the shell motif. The rhythmic Newport shell has deep plume-like waves that grow from a tight volute on either side of the lower edge. The Philadelphia interpretation offers a less rhythmic shell and volutes are usually separate from the body of the shell, flanking it instead.

Philadelphia makers constructed a seat frame out of three pieces of wood. A formed molding became the seat rim. The front leg was attached to the frame with one large dowel that came up, penetrating the frame at each corner. The side was then joined to the front rail and was pinned from the top on both sides of the dowel.

The roundabout, or corner chair, introduced in the previous period took on the new Queen Anne attributes. Turned legs were replaced with cabriole legs; back splats were incorporated and added a dimension of comfort for the sitter. Some models with deep front skirts hid a chamber pot or toilet device.

The easy chair began to take on regional traits. Boston and the larger New England area continued to make versions with arms that rolled out in a vertical manner. The new cabriole leg was included but many chairs still had not relinquished the dated stretchers. A well-documented Newport easy chair in the collection of New York's Metropolitan Museum of Art still retains its stunning original needlework upholstery.

Philadelphia also made these chairs with front cabriole legs and the Pennsylvania-associated feature of stump rear legs. They rarely had stretchers. The most distinguishing aspect was the C-scrolled arm, a more refined interpretation of the Queen Anne design theme.

The slipper chair, a new form, was intended for the bed chamber. Usually upholstered with a tall back, the chair stood on short legs. Some experts contend that this armless chair received its name because the sitter used it when putting on shoes; others believe the chair was designed to accommodate women of small stature.

Also new to the period were the sofa and settee, both of which reached the high point of their forms in Philadelphia. The sofa combined a long upholstered seat with a back and arms at each end. The sofa accommodated two or more people, and the name derives from the *sopha* of Eastern origin. It was popularized as the *canapé* in seventeenth-century France.

The Queen Anne version had an upholstered body that united a curvaceous back and arms with its seat. It stood on cabriole legs and looked to the curve of the high back and to the rolled curve of the arms to make a statement of beauty.

The settee, a lighter version of the sofa, was approximately double the width of a chair. The popularity of both pieces led to the gradual demise of the daybed, which in Queen Anne form was an extended version of the chair. The sofa reached a near-mainstream level of acceptance in the Federal period.

OPPOSITE PAGE: *This walnut and maple upholstered wing chair has the vertical rolled arms indicative of Massachusetts or Rhode Island, circa 1750. The cabriole legs ending in pad feet follow a Queen Anne idiom while the stretchers are retardataire, a stylistic holdover from earlier models.*

Still retaining its original elaborate needlework upholstery, this Newport easy chair is the marriage of comfort and high style.

Tables

Table forms developed in accord with changes in lifestyle. Social rituals such as tea drinking—now more affordable to a wider range of the population—and game playing necessitated the creation of special forms to facilitate these pastimes.

Just as Philadelphia makers were responsible for a stylistic high in chair design, New England craftsmen excelled in the making of the tea table. This form, introduced at the same time as the commodity for which it was named, was fabricated from walnut, cherry, or mahogany. Particularly fine examples have elongated, slender cabriole legs with well shaped ankles and pad feet. These pad feet occasionally topped even smaller circular flattened balls.

One example of the tea table so closely followed the English form—once removed from the Chinese—as to make them synonymous. This version resembled a tray on stand, with a square-dished top and relatively plain cabriole base.

Other versions began with cabriole legs that proceeded harmoniously to an arched skirt. Tops with a square surface had molded edges that integrated the design and protected the porcelain that sat on top from slippage. Connecticut cabinetmakers interpreted the Queen Anne curve to a stronger degree by scalloping the top to match the skirt.

Most of these tables lack carving, relying instead on the subtleties of balanced form and graceful line to set apart great examples from those of lesser pretense. The small scale of these tables points to their high degree of mobility.

Well-crafted tea tables from the middle colonies and from the South exist but they became a stylistic *tour de force* in the Chippendale period, especially in Philadelphia. Queen Anne tables from the South have straighter and sturdier legs and a more robust, bulbous club foot.

Mixing tables having walnut or mahogany frames covered with delft tiles or marble served decorative as well as practical purposes. These surfaces were more impervious to the liquor or beverage stains that mar so many similar tables with wood tops.

A documented Rhode Island example by John Goddard (1773–1785) with a mahogany frame and gray marble top remains a spectacular example of the form. Strong but graceful cabriole legs with pad feet support a daring serpentine frame.

Lacking applied ornament, the table is a tribute to Goddard's skill at uniting legs, frame, and serpentine top into something inherently sculptural. The table was constructed in 1755.

Although Newport furniture always revealed Baroque undertones, the highly sculptural essence of the piece alludes to high-style French taste and prefigures a Rococo influence in traditional Newport understatement.

Drop-leaf tables supplanted gate-leg tables of the past. Instead of stretchers, Queen Anne drop leaves were made with four cabriole legs, two of which were stationary. The other two were attached to rails that swung, earning these tables the alternate name of swing-leg tables. Extra-large tables might have four swing legs.

With some variation, most tops measure from three to five and a half feet (90–165 cm) when extended. Crafted by the same makers who produced chairs, and serving a multiplicity of purposes, these tables were both used domestically and exported. Lacking stretchers and dependent on thinner cabriole legs, drop-leaf tables are more fragile than their earlier gate-leg counterparts.

Inventories show that drop-leaf tables were used foremost as dining tables, but it wasn't uncommon for them to be used as writing tables. When in service the top was cov-

OPPOSITE PAGE: *The simple design of this Newport mahogany tea table resembling a tray on a stand is derived from earlier Chinese models. The pointed slipper feet are characteristic of the Goddard-Townsend School.* **RIGHT:** *Even more provincial pieces such as this tavern table of maple with old red paint over the original green understood the message of Hogarth's "line of beauty." This table with cyma scrolling is from Connecticut, circa 1730 to 1750.*

ered with a cloth; when not in service the leaves were dropped and the table was stored against a wall. This usage followed century-old conventions.

Some drop-leaf tables were made with drawers, but those tables with two stationary legs usually were not. Turned-leg tables had round or oval tops that were secured to the frame with wooden pins. Cabriole models had tops that were attached with invisible fasteners such as screws through the frame into the top or into blocks glued to the frame.

Ovolo moldings finished the edges of these tabletops where straight or rounded edges once prevailed. The ovolo is a convex molding, most often a quarter circle in profile. This attention to detail—and the inclusion of a shape sometimes associated with Renaissance design— underscores the preoccupation with order and proportion that ruled this age.

The increased leisure time associated with a prosperous merchant class served as the impetus behind the development of the card table. In form, most examples are rectangular in shape and possess a swing leg that supports the top in an opened position. Dished compartments called "guinea holes" or "fish ponds" were used for counters, and dished corners for candlestands often show up on these tables. Cabriole legs were finished with claw-and-ball or pad feet.

Massachusetts examples display the same delicacy as tea tables from the region, with poised legs, well-defined ankles, and good proportions. Two of the finest examples of card tables on public display are those in the collection of the Museum of Fine Arts in Boston.

Both have needlework tops—especially valuable since less than six such tables with original canvaswork playing surfaces remain. One reason for the relatively undisturbed condition of the needlework owes to the folding lids that shield them from light.

Oval-shaped tops on card tables are rare in American Queen Anne work. One of these examples sports an oval top but it was probably based on a variant of an English card table. The other example (although probably made in England) appealed to colonial Bostonians still looking to England for guidance in the arts.

The Massachusetts oval-topped table features a colorfully worked outer band of cards and gaming paraphernalia circling a center of floral sprays, uniting the oval infrastructure of the walnut base with its decorative playing surface. Standing on cabriole legs that are finished with claw-and-ball feet, the table's rear leg pulls out of a slot in the frame. The pull-out leg differs slightly from standard swing leg construction.

The English example, made of mahogany with pine, has a squared top with rounded turret corners. Its legs are

hinged, another deviation from the standard swing leg.

The most fascinating feature of the squared-top table is the needlework playing surface. It pictures a woman lost in reverie reclining against a tree. A distant town, flowers, foliage, birds, and a man surround her. The composition parallels English prints and embroideries of the mid-eighteenth century.

Like the distance between the woman and the town, the picture illustrates how far removed this woman was from the trials of everyday life. It depicts a concern for leisure that would have been a foreign concept in earlier decades.

Card tables from the South often followed English and Irish prototypes. Table legs follow the local tendency to form a stout stance and to have less clearly delineated ankles. Many have a sturdiness lacking in New England examples.

The tilt-top table, or a table hinged to a base enabling it to tip to a vertical position, is the modern term for a table known by many period names. The English traditionally

referred to them as pillar-and-claw or claw tables, regardless of whether the table had claw-and-ball feet. Many colonial cabinetmakers simply called them tea tables. Collectors often look to the decorative flourishes of the pillar in assessing the desirability of a particular example.

The most prolific shape, the round tilt-top, was connected to a pillar or column that ended in a base with short tripod cabriole legs. Second in popularity was the square top with rounded or serpentine edges. Philadelphia models made use of a birdcage device between the top and the pillar that permitted the top to tilt and rotate.

Depending on shop practice and on consumer preference, feet were of the claw-and-ball or snake variety. The snake foot, usually found on tables from the north shore of Massachusetts, takes its name from the shape of the swelled curves that resembles a snake's head. Tables with the claw-and-ball foot appealed to Philadelphia taste, and usually had a dished top. Adding such labor-intensive details tended to increase the final cost.

Bedsteads

edsteads dating from 1725 to 1760 followed earlier precedent; they were simple frames designed to wear the elaborate textiles of the period. The typical bed found in an upscale home would be thickly draped with fabric. A tester, or canopy of a four-post or draped bed, held valances on the sides and a head-cloth that draped behind pillows.

Panels or curtains hanging from the tester to the floor could be closed at night for an additional measure of warmth. A matching coverlet and bases totally enveloped the bed in cloth. Some models had short cabriole legs, but few of these models survive.

The field bed, a canopy bed of smaller scale, was based on portable beds purportedly used by the military. Compared to the large fabric-draped models, the field bed usually has low turned posts and an arched canopy.

Fabric for the bed fashions continued to be imported. But with the increase in leisure activities and attention to developing social graces that characterized the time, fancy needlework done by women and school girls often supplied the decorative detail and charm.

Those who wished to demonstrate fancy needlework skills—the mark of a woman's refinement and talents enriched through the pursuit of leisure—bought imported English fabrics with designs laid out on the surface that they completed. The quality of the work, in addition to the fabric and yarn, is another important memento of colonial material culture.

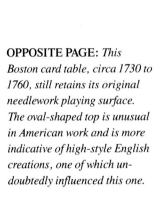

OPPOSITE PAGE: *This Boston card table, circa 1730 to 1760, still retains its original needlework playing surface. The oval-shaped top is unusual in American work and is more indicative of high-style English creations, one of which undoubtedly influenced this one.*

The folding bed was a necessity in a smaller colonial home since rooms continued to serve multiple purposes. When not in use, the bed was pushed against a wall with the frame folded up.

Chippendale Furniture

(1755–1790)

There is scarce a room where one does not see the waving-line employ'd in some way or other. How inelegant would the shapes of all our moveables be without it?...

William Hogarth,
The Analysis of Beauty, 1753

These words helped to introduce the Rococo, or modern French style, to the colonies. Along with the taste for Chinese and Gothic novelties, it formed the basis of the Chippendale style in America.

As these international stylistic crosscurrents met, the economic and political clout of the colonies was expanding at a frenzied pace. Colonial population doubled in size roughly every twenty years. A building boom continued throughout the colonies, interrupted only by the Revolution.

Far from the closed societies of England and the Continent, in the colonies the names of newly prosperous families were constantly updating the rosters. Philadelphia had grown into one of the largest and most progressive cities. Its population tripled in the quarter-century before the Revolution.

Charleston, too, had become an exciting city, and by the standards of the late eighteenth century, a cultivated one as well. Baltimore, which would rise to economic significance following the Revolution, began its climb to maturity during this period. Annapolis was also growing, and would become the "Athens of America" at about the time of the Revolution.

Adam Smith, the Scottish political economist whose work became the foundation upon which English classical economics was founded, observed: "England purchased for some of her subjects, who found themselves uneasy at home, a great estate in a distant country." This possessive attitude determined England's stance toward her colonial dominion from the beginning.

Political and economic theory held that the colonies were expected to be primary providers of cheap raw materials on the supply side, and consumers of costly finished goods on the demand side, resulting in a balance of trade that heavily favored England. As a premise of the mercantile formula, one country's gain usually meant a

trading loss to its partners. This situation created and sharpened economic rivalries.

England by this time had enacted a series of laws, including the Acts of Trade and Navigation, that prohibited the colonies from importing goods from sources other than England. The driving force behind such restrictions was the goal of dissuading any "errors of independency." The despised Stamp Act of 1765 acted as another irritant to colonists already chafing at restrictions. As Britain attempted to control the growing colonial mercantile economy, colonists countered with nonimportation agreements.

Despite a growing dissatisfaction with their economic and political status vis-à-vis England, colonial Americans continued to be linked to the material culture and to the larger web of English society. Indeed, during this time it became fashionable for wealthy colonists to travel back to England to conduct business or to follow more intellectual quests in education and in the arts.

Many artists in the fine arts, following the lead of the expatriate Benjamin West, travelled to England. Even the doyenne of colonial portraiture, John Singleton Copley, felt the urge to make the trip as a way to refine his technique. These scholarly and intellectual activities culminated in the "Grand Tour," a voyage to England and the Continent made by every culturally refined colonist. Such trips paused for the Revolution then resumed at its conclusion, and continued well into the mid-nineteenth century.

Little did England's rulers realize how the ideas of the Enlightenment, only marginally influential in Europe, would set ablaze in the colonies an ideological and practical desire to be free of the heavy burdens of Mother England. When combined with economic and political dissatisfaction, the result was the Revolution. These events forever changed the course of world history, and the discussion that follows reflects these changes.

Courtesy The Metropolitan Museum of Art, NYC, Rogers Fund, 1918/photo by Richard Cheek

Style Overview

By this point in the development of American colonial furniture, it should come as no surprise that the term Chippendale furniture is another convenient catch-all phrase for a certain aesthetic that is more multifarious than the individual for whom it was named. The Chippendale aesthetic prevailed in the colonies from the mid-eighteenth century until about the time of the American Revolution. Its primary influence was the Rococo, which was often mixed capriciously with Chinese and Gothic novelties to form what is loosely called the Chippendale style.

The major component of the style was the Rococo element. Rococo developed in the eighteenth century as a reaction to the classically derived imperatives of late Baroque design. Originating in France under the reign of Louis XV, it is characterized by lightened, curved, and irregular forms ornamented by naturalistic and organic shapes. *Rocailles,* or rocks, and *coquilles,* or shells, often provided decorative surface ornament for the underlying curved forms.

Paradoxically, the name Rococo was itself coined after the style originally had its debut. A bastardization of *rocaille* and *coquille,* the term first surfaced in nineteenth-century France and was adopted by students of the academic artist Jacques-Louis David as a way to deride what these emerging neo-classicists believed was an overtly sensual and frivolous message.

A look at how this style took hold across Europe will help explain its last stage manifestation in the colonies.

The Rococo style was international in scope, developing simultaneously with a desire for gracious and intimate living. And while this penchant had long dictated much of court life, for the first time the bourgeoisie adopted it as a coveted lifestyle. This would prove particularly important in the growing fascination with the Rococo that surfaced in England and in the colonies.

England during this period was prospering. The landed gentry, together with the banking and mercantile conglomerates, wielded an economic clout that rivalled that of the Crown. The English court became removed from the popular taste, and exerted little influence on the growing popularity of Rococo style.

It was the immensely affluent Whigs who established a taste for the Rococo in England. They, through their cabinetmakers, diluted Rococo's French opulence into a typically understated English blueprint that was more practical than sumptuous.

At the heart of this English reserve was a difference in patterns of living. French society was dominated by women; in English culture society never fully emerged from male control. Likewise, in English decor, the feminine influence was usually limited to dressing rooms or to bed chambers.

When the Rococo wave washed ashore in England it was manifested as more of a decorative surface embellishment than a full blown sea of feminine, irregular forms and organic ornament. These factors, combined with the threat France always presented to England's colonial trade, helped to soften the influence that French designers would exert on the English furniture industry.

Stylistically, the Rococo was introduced and taught in England at the Academy of St. Martin's Lane, founded by William Hogarth. The French painter H. F. Gravelot taught students the rudiments of Rococo ornamentation.

When closed, this Massachusetts mahogany drop-leaf table, circa 1770, has a high degree of portability. The gracefully shaped aprons at either end are desirable as are the well-articulated claw-and-ball feet.

The visual impact of this graduated four-drawer chest from the Delaware Valley is achieved through the use of tiger maple. It stands on straight bracket feet, one of several popular shapes for Chippendale case pieces.

Courtesy C.L. Prickett, Yardely, PA

toire of Rococo design elements, Thomas Chippendale's 1754 publication, *The Gentleman and Cabinet-Maker's Director,* was perhaps the best-timed and certainly the most influential. Its 161 plates depicted nearly every furniture form in 200 plates by its third edition in 1762.

In addition to publicizing the Rococo, Chippendale is to be applauded for his efforts at establishing a comprehensive source of design ideas that could be successfully imposed on more indigenous English forms.

The success of the *Director* reveals the importance of design books in the period. From the Renaissance through the nineteenth century, drawing was the medium from which many decorative arts descended. Today, these drawings are collectibles in their own right.

Thus, Chippendale's work was monumentally important to those colonial craftsmen and their patrons who hungered for fashionable British style yet wished to patronize colonial products. It was fashion without guilt.

English design never threatened to replace French achievements in the theater of Rococo mannerism. An English Rococo looking glass never achieved the playful and sensuous asymmetry of its French prototype. But in his more domesticated interpretation, Chippendale laid out French design with Gothic and Chinese decorative enhancements so successfully that the *Director* became the shorthand for these three stylistic crosscurrents, and had a massive impact on American colonial furniture covering the years of 1755 to 1790.

Chippendale's French or "modern" illustrations borrowed elements of Rococo ornament, including ribbons, rocks, and shells. These were applied to underlying forms. Where in France, asymmetrical and curvaceous shapes were more popular, England held fast to more restrained and classical shape and proportion. This, in turn, yielded a product that found its way into similarly restrained colonial versions.

The interest in the ornamental styles of the Far East that began in the William and Mary period continued with slight modifications. Motifs that once focused on bamboo and peonies moved toward the more exotic Rococo images of roses and acanthus; dragons were transformed into birds. *Chinoiserie* is the name given to the Western interpretation of Oriental motifs.

Mahogany pieces included Oriental fretwork, openwork patterns of lines formed by a fretsaw. Pagoda tops were another device that recalled things Oriental. Some pieces amalgamated fantasies of Oriental, Rococo, and classical detail in a single item.

Craftsmen and cabinetmakers learned the Rococo formula through various design and drawing classes. English furniture conceived with this Rococo inspiration is sometimes referred to as the "St. Martin's Lane style."

Although it was not the first treatise to describe a reper-

The last of the major components of Chippendale's decorative orgy was the Gothic element, a style that was the most indigenous of the three. To separate this revival-like style from the original Gothic that was based on structural and decorative tendencies that prevailed in Christian Europe before the Renaissance, and from the Gothic Revival style that surfaced later in the nineteenth century through the work of Pugin, English antiquarians occasionally refer to the mid-eighteenth style as the *Gothick* or *faux-gothique* style.

A logical outgrowth of England's domestic focus in early eighteenth-century furniture design, the Gothic style got its start in the 1730s. The English version of this style, like its counterparts above, was essentially one of detail rather than form, evoking the spirit of medieval design but not its historical accuracy.

Details such as pointed arches and quatrefoils were applied with a more frivolous abandon; elements were mixed from differing historic intervals within the Gothic framework. Horace Walpole's house, Strawberry Hill, recalled England's strong medieval heritage but in a less serious vein.

Courtesy Northeast Auctions, Hampton, NH

In England, the Gothic style was best suited to the typically masculine domain of the library, and it reiterated the religious, intellectual, and masculine association that the style originally found in the architecture of medieval Europe. Chippendale's designs subsequently illustrated bookcases with this type of decorative detail.

As England looked to its past, colonial America looked even more closely to England in the period before the Revolution in matters of style and taste in the arts. The Chippendale style arrived in the colonies in three ways: through the skills of recent immigrants, the importation of English pieces, and the use of pattern books.

Immigrant craftsmen brought their knowledge of Chippendale style with them. Advertisements from the period cited these purveyors as being "late of London." Wealthy colonial potentates, like their bourgeoisie Whig brethren, were only too eager to succumb to this marketing ploy when selecting a cabinetmaker as a way to reflect their avant-garde taste.

Of course, actual Chippendale pieces also made their way to the colonies as some English-made furniture was exported. Most of these went to the South, although the numbers diminished as the century progressed.

In 1765, Samuel Powel was advised by his uncle not to return from London with a shipment of English furniture: "Household goods may be had here as cheap and as well made from English patterns... In the humour people are in here, a man is in danger of becoming Invidiously distinguished, who buys anything in England which our Tradesmen can furnish...."

The mahogany and gilt looking glass from Massachusetts, circa 1770, has an organic vine motif. The tall case clock from New Jersey, circa 1785, *projects a sense of movement. The fluted quarter columns and acanthus-carved cabriole legs of the lowboy are the summit of Philadelphia work, circa 1765.*

Courtesy C.L. Prickett, Yardley, PA

While patriotic colonists afraid of being labelled "Tory" began to look disapprovingly on the importation of English merchandise that might be readily procured in the colonies, the flow of ideas did not stop with the cessation of imports. Pattern books, the most effective source of design migration, reinforced colonial artistic dependency on an English idiom but not at the expense of the colonial cabinetmakers.

Chippendale's *Director* circulated rapidly among colonial cabinetmakers. Philadelphia and Charleston craftsmen fell most strongly under its spell while conservative New England—particularly Newport—held on to late Baroque form, perhaps incorporating some modern ornament. Based on period newspapers, Philadelphia ordered the largest number of copies of the *Director* while Newport ordered the fewest.

By all accounts, the colonial response to Rococo excess was—as it had been in England—to adopt ornament instead of form. The colonies adapted and personalized the design components that Chippendale had formalized.

Like colonial furniture styles that preceded it, American Chippendale furniture design was of British parentage yet possessed a distinctive personality of its own. Through a studied yet independent arrangement of elements, craftsmen turned out uniquely colonial products with many distinct regional characteristics.

In the Chippendale period, the graceful curve of the Queen Anne style became more pronounced and angled. Chair crests sprouted ears, and plain vase-shaped splats were transformed into pierced and carved displays of woodworking prowess. Unlike French Rococo case pieces, most colonial furniture retained the architectural form that proved so successful in Queen Anne designs.

Cabinetmakers added sophisticated carved foliate ornament and cartouches to update styles. Bonnet-top high chests were represented as having "crown and claws."

OPPOSITE PAGE, TOP: *Brasses with a free-form design complement the figured mahogany body of this beautifully orchestrated Massachusetts oxbow chest. The moveable oxbow front provides the sense of movement so important to successful Chippendale design.*

ABOVE: *Following eighteenth-century convention, rooms often mixed furniture from several stylistic intervals. Pictured here is a Queen Anne drop-leaf table surrounded by Massachusetts Chippendale chairs.*

Some case pieces emphasized Rococo adornments to a stronger degree; swelled or blocked surfaces, serpentine and oxbow fronts added another layer of curvilinear appeal. These exceptions brought colonists one step closer to the sensuality of French design.

The cabriole leg with claw-and-ball foot continued to be a distinctive colonial trait into the Chippendale period, even though its popularity in England had waned, and even though Chippendale's *Director* ignored it completely.

Regional characteristics became highly defined in legs and feet in major style centers and provide important clues to regional preferences and shop practices. Many of these characteristics were magnified thanks to shop practices that were carefully regulated and dominated by master artisans who perpetuated these traditions with a system of apprenticeships. It is important to remember, however, that such traits are guidelines, not necessarily dogma, for there are examples of crossfertilization of components throughout American furniture.

A Massachusetts claw-and-ball foot has a typically high ball with slender talons that are swept back. In side view, the talons often form a triangle. A Newport claw-and-ball has crisp, elongated talons that curve away from the ball, often resulting in the most unique of all the designs, and it is called an undercut talon. Some models have webbing between the toes.

A Connecticut claw-and-ball, conversely, has broader talons that might be roughly carved. In Philadelphia, the claw-and-ball foot was well carved with a sturdy claw that holds a flattened ball. New York versions are often flatter in the ball and are rather boxy in shape.

Regional carving differences show in the knees as well. In Newport, knee carving was as stylized as foot carving. Specifically, it was flat and resembled *intaglio,* or a carved design that is cut into a surface rather than being raised from it.

Knee carving in Massachusetts often showed acanthus leaves rendered in a flat and slightly stiff manner. In New York, the preference was for flat acanthus carving, often with cross-hatching in the center of the knee. Philadelphia knees were well rounded, fluidly carved, and sometimes contained two-part foliage that met in the center of the knee.

Chippendale offered options such as the French scroll foot, or whorl foot. The Marlborough leg, a square leg sometimes terminating in a blocked foot, was another period variant that worked particularly well with the more angular Gothic and Chinese styles.

The Age of Reason created a demand for intellectual

This Chippendale carved mahogany side chair has stump rear legs, which is characteristic of Philadelphia origin. The masterfully carved shells on the ears as well as the acanthus-carved legs with claw-and-ball feet are notable.

order and symmetry. England and colonial America followed this dictum to the strongest degree while France and much of Europe delighted in the curved forms that evaded classically proportioned elements.

Even in the most ambitious of colonial designs, classical proportions and quarter columns prevailed on case pieces. Surprisingly, Chippendale's *Director* reaffirmed that: "Of all the Arts which are either improved or ornamented by Architecture, that of Cabinet-Making is not only the most useful and ornamental, but capable of receiving as great Assistance from it as any whatever."

In the choice of materials, imported mahogany rose to become the preferred wood in Chippendale furniture. At least three factors combined to assure mahogany's first place status.

Richly figured mahogany was more suitable to Rococo's dazzling surfaces. Its use would prove especially important in the colonies: Because it lacked the zealous displays of European glitter, colonial furniture came to depend on the open grain of the wood to contrast with the more confining infrastructure.

Mahogany was the strongest of materials. It lent itself well to the intricate and often precarious nature of interlaced fabrication and carving. More demands were placed on the wood since thinner splats interacted with greater voids. Mahogany met this challenge easily.

Lastly, mahogany was all but impervious to insects. This alone made it a natural choice for the warm and humid climate of Charleston as well as for those more tropical climates to which pieces made from it were exported.

The durability of the wood encouraged carvers to experiment with a multiplicity of motifs, including swirls, scrolls, foliage, and shells.

Chair carving was usually confined to the cabriole leg and foot and to the crest rail and splat. Regional carving styles, as outlined above, become easily recognizable with some practice.

Beyond the utilitarian function they performed, brasses attached to a piece served to visually organize an object, uniting its various components into a coherent whole. In dark rooms, the light that danced off their highly polished surfaces provided a measure of Rococo *joie de vivre.*

Pulls ranged from simple bail handles that resembled a flattened U-shape to flattened but meandering urn brasses with a bail handle that reflected the open and flowing message of Chippendale taste. Other pulls matched chair splats in the intricacy of their cut-out patterns. Stylistically the latest, these cut-out patterns entertained the eye and were a delightful blending of Rococo, Gothic, and Chinese patterns that blurred the distinction between the three.

Although the colonies had no formal guilds that compared to those of England and the Continent, groups of cabinetmakers and their apprentices adhered to strict shop guidelines that came as close to a guild as was practical. Therefore, the growing habit of labelling and otherwise marking furniture that began in these years was a logical step in the development of colonial cabinetmaking.

Courtesy Leigh Keno, NYC (both photos)

ABOVE: *Authenticated to the workshop of John Goddard of Newport, Rhode Island, 1760 to 1775, this mahogany card table makes an important statement about restrained Chippendale design.* **BELOW:** *When open, the table reveals a dished-out felt-covered playing surface and four carved candle recesses. The front legs terminate in claw-and-ball feet with undercut talons and the rear legs end in pad-and-disk feet, all characteristic of Goddard-Townsend pieces.*

Case Pieces

athaniel Hawthorne wrote: "After all, the moderns have invented nothing better in chamber furniture than those chests which stand on four slender legs, and send an absolute tower of mahogany to the ceiling, the whole terminating in a fantastically carved ornament."

If there was a peculiarly colonial furniture form, it was the high chest. While the form had appeared in England, it never achieved the height of popularity that it did in the colonies. About the time English cabinetmakers decried the form as all but obsolete, colonial craftsmen were immortalizing it, especially in Philadelphia.

In form alone, late colonial Philadelphia high chests were holdovers from the architectural view that demanded respect for classical order. Swan-neck or broken-scroll pediments, admittedly more freely executed, helped augment Hogarth's line of beauty.

The French were intellectually able to leave behind the tight and rigidly defined five orders. Colonial artisans, mirroring English design sources, were not. Most Philadelphia high chests, therefore, continued to incorporate slender quarter columns on the front of case pieces, characteristic of the Doric Order.

If Philadelphia represented the most advanced center of Chippendale design, then it is understandable that more conservative New England locales continued to produce furniture with a Baroque flavor. This is particularly noticeable in the pediments on case pieces.

If one were to connect the invisible lines that move from the corners of the pediment to the center of the pediment, a triangle emerges. The triangle is the most stable of forms and was a major component of classical art.

Mahogany was selected based on its ability to excite the eye through figuring that helped to break the confines of the chest's underlying form, if only suggestively. Carving could be as subdued as some of the relatively plain designs employed by the furniture maker William Savery (1721–1788). Probably appealing to a Quaker aesthetic, to a more modest pocketbook, or to a combination of both, a William Savery chest was plain by many a Philadelphian's standards.

Cabriole knees and skirts with simple scrolled carving, claw-and-ball feet, and a pierced scrolled bonnet that ends

Courtesy The Metropolitan Museum of Art, NYC, John Stewart Kennedy Fund, 1918

ABOVE: *One of the most sophisticated high chests ever designed, this exquisitely proportioned piece endures as an example of Philadelphia taste. The materials and workmanship are of the highest order.* **OPPOSITE PAGE:** *This Connecticut cherry high chest by Philadelphia-trained Eliphalet Chapin borrowed the proportions, cabriole leg, skirt and cut-out lattice pattern, and "sea horse" cartouche from dressier Philadelphia models, adapting them to a more conservative Connecticut clientele.*

in rosettes and three urn finials describe the body. Drawer pulls made of bails attached to urns were the fanciest component.

By contrast, a Philadelphia high chest known as the "Pompadour highboy" for the bust that sits atop the piece, bursts with carved detail that in its fluidity leads the eye somewhat astray from the underlying squared form. The bust supposedly resembles the head of Louis XV's mistress, but its inclusion is more indicative of Rococo theatrical effect than historical accuracy. On view at New York's Metropolitan Museum of Art, the chest is as much a showstopper now as it must have been in the best chamber of an eighteenth-century house.

The case is supported by sturdy, well-proportioned cabriole legs that end in the claw-and-ball feet characteristic of the area. Dated 1765 to 1775, this chest's five tiers of drawers over a two-tier base is another clue to its Philadelphia origin.

One of the most intricately carved examples of the form, it boasts organic and representational motifs. For America, the carving was unabashedly Rococo, but it was decidedly more restrained than that of its French forebears.

Acanthus leaves and other flora meander over the legs and skirt and reach a bold display in the open scroll of the pediment. Huge acanthus leaves swirl out of the pediment.

The free-form shapes of the carving make this piece perhaps the closest American rendition of modern French taste. The quality of execution is superlative. On less important models this carving would appear flatter, possibly indicating that the carver was trying to copy the pattern from a book.

The quarter columns are smothered with scrolled details while the top just beneath the cornice and the waist or mid-section cut-out carvings resemble fretwork. This combination of Rococo detail with a repetitive pattern that is vaguely Oriental was indicative of how disparate elements were commingled in the Chippendale era.

The maker borrowed heavily from Chippendale's *Director*. The draped urns, so redolent of the classical, stand proudly on top of the pediment almost in defiance of the Rococo-inspired organic carving. These, along with the scene on the bottom drawer that is believed to represent one of Aesop's fables, both have origins in the *Director*.

U-shaped bails secured through organic looking mounts complete the decorative portrait. Still extant is the matching low boy or dressing table. Singly or together these pieces demonstrate a product turned out by a highly specialized team. They are inestimable as tools of late colonial material erudition.

In Newport, another Quaker city, cabinetmakers couldn't have construed the high chest more differently. The Newport high chest lost the pointed slipper feet of earlier models. Squared knees were retained, and claw-and-ball feet with undercut talons frequently replaced slipper feet. Rear legs sometimes ended in simple turned pad feet.

When compared to a Philadelphia version, a Newport high chest is serene and quiet. In form, the Newport chest is more tightly configured. This is evident in just about

Even the finials show this tightness. The cupcake finial, usually attributed to the Goddard–Townsend shops, is a tautly spiralled flame resting on a fluted cupcake-shaped base. A carved undulating shell moves with the rhythm of the skirt. The desk and bookcase began to replace the high chest, which was reaching its peak popularity in Newport.

The Quaker communities of Philadelphia and Newport present somewhat of a puzzle—it is difficult to determine all the forces that were at work that so influenced Philadelphia to adopt such a strong Rococo edict and Newport to retain older Baroque forms.

The demographics of the areas may yield some clues. Philadelphia was a growing city with a distinct nouveau-riche attitude and it was the second most influential city of its time, next to Boston. Immigrants from London, Ireland, and Scotland flocked to Philadelphia, bringing the latest styles with them. In contrast, Newport was a smaller, more conservative city. Further, the closed nature of the Newport group of cabinetmakers was significant. The Goddard–Townsend shops regulated and influenced consumption patterns to a degree that a single cabinetmaker could not match. Regardless of what forces shaped the stylistic preferences of these two locales, both designs are to be cherished, one for a sculptural beauty, the other for its more decorative appeal.

As in the Queen Anne period, Connecticut Chippendale furniture fell under the stylistic sway of many areas, including the diverse regions of Philadelphia, Rhode Island, and Massachusetts. In Connecticut, for example, the Newport shell was transformed from an exceptionally undulating shape to one that was noticeably more staid and less crisp.

There are regional differences, however, even between Connecticut examples. For example, Norwich, Connecticut, pieces followed the Newport lead, while pieces from the Hartford area were often more closely aligned with the styles of Philadelphia, Boston, Salem, and New York.

Consequently, there is no single set of qualities that typifies Connecticut work, especially when the more inventive designs of local Connecticut makers are factored into the scenario.

Eliphalet Chapin (1741–1807) of East Windsor, Connecticut, stands out as one cabinetmaker whose work mixed regional elements. Chapin moved to Connecticut after working in Philadelphia for four years.

He formulated a homogeneous style using cherry and certain Philadelphia structural and decorative techniques that produced highly individual pieces. Through his

ABOVE: *The open-flame finials on this Philadelphia high chest contrast with the tightly spiralled versions on New England cases. The cartouche and cabochon center finial, the fluid carving, and the sturdy claw grasping a flattened ball bespeak Philadelphia craftsmanship.*

OPPOSITE PAGE: *The fretwork frieze that adorns the split top drawer on this mahogany chest is a decorative nuance found on finer examples of Philadelphia case work. The fluted quarter columns and curved ogee bracket feet surpass standard fare.*

every detail. The grain of mahogany, for example, is less highly figured. The brasses, while forming typical Chippendale patterns, are highly symmetrical and tight. It was customary by this time to mount large carrying brasses on the sides of many cases.

Quarter columns are fluted, further emphasizing a linear quality. The scalloped bonnet is extended or filled in to the rear of the upper case. This contrasts strongly with the Philadelphia chest, on which the bonnet is merely a facade.

efforts and through those of the apprentices he trained, the Philadelphia style found its way to Connecticut. The Wadsworth Atheneum in Hartford, Connecticut, houses a high chest attributed to him.

Dated between 1771 and 1795, Chapin's high chest shares the proportions, cabriole leg, skirt, and cut-out lattice pattern of the scrolled bonnet and asymmetrical, "sea horse" cartouche that typify high-style Philadelphia chests. On the other hand, there is a delicacy to the chest that is obvious in the vine ornament that sparingly graces the upper and lower drawers.

The light cartouche and vine ornament bespeak Philadelphia Rococo motifs in a uniquely Connecticut format. The combination of these details, the choice of cherry and white pine, and the use of shaped finials were intended to capture the more conservative eye of the Connecticut patron.

The Dunlap family from southern New Hampshire was another circle of cabinetmakers whose style was distinctive. John (1746–1792), was joined by his brother, Samuel (1752–1820), and his four nephews in this endeavor. The Dunlap family's work is known for its idiosyncratic variety of Chippendale ornamentation.

A high chest of drawers produced by this group used maple and soft white pine instead of mahogany, some of it stained to resemble the costly imported commodity. The proportionally short and slender cabriole legs have creased knees that end in claw-and-ball feet or in pad feet built up from angled disks. Many of these pieces have a top-heavy look since they stand on short legs.

One configuration called for a top case of five or more tiers of drawers over a lower case of three tiers of drawers. The skirt is an imaginative blend of curves and shells. A deep cornice was topped with a pierced basket-weave band of fan carving modified with small broken scroll pediments.

The carved fans are sometimes called "spoonhandles" for the spread out ray shapes that resemble the handles of a spoon. They are another example of a regional hand at work, probably influenced by the stylized Newport shell.

Chippendale brasses appear on most models, although some chests show evidence of original oval brasses typical of Federal taste. Most of these chests date from the last quarter of the eighteenth century.

It appears that New York craftsmen made the least number of high chests in the Chippendale years. Cabinetmakers and their benefactors instead opted for the chest-on-chest, which was popular in England.

The New York high chest was more likely to have a flat top with an architectural cornice. Dimensions were laid out in a square case, usually with fluted and chamfered corners. Cabriole legs and a scalloped skirt soften the simple design. Sweet gum, a favored choice of New York makers, occasionally substituted for mahogany.

New Yorkers preferred the chest-on-chest or the linen press for storage. Most New York examples of these forms closely follow English archetypes. This form was also made in Philadelphia, even though cabinetmakers there were preoccupied with the scrolled-top high chest.

Allowing for subtle ornamental peculiarities, most of these chests were architectural in form. Columns and flat cornices enhanced with dentil moldings outlined frames. Ogee bracket feet were a welcome change from cabriole legs on some examples. The ogee bracket was a cyma reverse profile curve. The short stocky foot provided a visually stable base upon which the case could rest.

Charleston examples follow English format almost exclusively and were built from mahogany or local walnut. Cantered corners and complicated fretwork are often associated with London-born cabinetmaker Thomas Elfe (active 1747–1775) who was Charleston's foremost furniture maker during the period.

Elfe, trained in England, was responsible for much, but not all, sophisticated Charleston furniture. Recent study is less vociferous in attributing all pieces with these characteristics to Elfe, instead ascribing them to Charleston workmanship in general. Study of southern furniture has sometimes been hampered by the fact that many slaves worked in the trade and their names have remained unknown.

So strong was Charleston's allegiance to English taste that a library bookcase, a rare colonial form, made in Charleston between 1755 and 1775 copies almost line for line Plate 93 of the 1754 edition of Chippendale's *Director.* The nearly one hundred six-inch (265-cm) tall bookcase, now part of the collection of the Museum of Early Southern Decorative Arts in Winston-Salem, North Carolina, is one of the most inspiring of eighteenth-century designs.

Two smaller sections flank a larger and taller midsection. The top sections hold shelves that are protected by glass that has been decoratively outlined in the midsection with a stylized Gothic motif. Chippendale was fond of this motif for the libraries where such a piece might appear.

The flanking two sections have a French motif, and when combined with the design on the midsection, illustrate how

pieces could conceivably integrate motifs from one, two, or all three of Chippendale's suggested components.

The bottom case is defined by fret and inlay; the base stands on bracket feet. The two side sections form a double arch pediment that is divided by the triangular pediment of the center compartment. When combined with a clearly outlined and linear base, the overall geometric shape of the piece shines through.

New England evinced a growing affection for large case pieces, particularly the desk and bookcase. Philadelphia has historically been applauded as the center of highest Rococo spirit in the colonies while New England supposedly clung to the old Queen Anne style. If one is guided by the premise that the Rococo spirit was essentially one of a decorative vocabulary, then this statement is accurate.

If, however, one brings to the debate a thorough grounding of the true Rococo mode as expressed in France—

A rare colonial form, this mahogany library bookcase from Charleston, South Carolina, reveals the city's strong ties to English design. This model is nearly identical to a rendering in Chippendale's Director. **OPPOSITE PAGE:** *The oxbow blocking, double ogee bracket feet, and bold overhang all combine to lend a sculptural quality to this cherry bureau from Connecticut, circa 1760 to 1780. The drawers retain their original brasses.*

its primary source—then New England cabinet pieces, especially those from Boston and Salem, would come to the forefront of Rococo design both in form and in ornament.

A Boston chest-on-chest signed "John Cogswell, Middle Street, Boston, 1782" surpasses its Philadelphia counterparts in many ways but most dramatically in its advanced form.

The resplendent chest rests on a bombé or kettle-shaped base. With its outward bulging sides and front the piece gives credit to a wider Rococo heritage than some of its Philadelphia equivalents.

Specifically, the base in its swollen form acknowledges the curvilinear aspect of the French Rococo in a way that Philadelphia cases never did. Rich mahogany provided a backdrop for Chippendale-style brasses (replaced), fluted pilasters or flattened columns, and a melange of robust carving.

The open scrolled pediment punctuated with free-form rosettes and flowing foliage merges with fretwork to unify the creation, revealing the maker's understanding of how the varied elements of Chippendale style could be fused in a single beautiful and functional object.

The crowning glory is a gilded eagle that perches on top of a finial, predicting the eagle motif that would become de rigueur in the Federal period.

The Goddard–Townsend shops perfected the desk and bookcase to an extent that was nearly unequalled in the colonies. This form became the *pièce de resistance* in the late eighteenth century, and institutions such as the Metropolitan Museum, Winterthur, and the Boston Museum of Fine Arts lovingly display three remaining examples.

In form, these cases represent a continuation of Queen Anne proportion and architectural undertones while advancing the technique of the blocked or "sweld" facade. This is not unexpected, as conservative Newport did not get swept up in the great wave of the Rococo as did its sister city Philadelphia.

The mahogany facade was blocked into three sections, two convex and one concave. The block extends from the door panels on the top case all the way down through the base. Ogee bracket feet possess another Newport feature —a small scroll on the inside of the foot.

These surfaces were cut from solid blocks of wood, creating an overall effect that was immensely sculptural. The warm mahogany and the undulating panels dispensed enough interest so that little additional ornament was necessary.

Discreet fluted Doric quarter colonnettes prevent the eye from wandering too far off the surface and help reorient the eye vertically. A scrolled pediment is accentuated with three cupcake finials.

Three shells adorn the top blocked panels and three adorn the fall-front board of the desk. This created a marked contrast of planes. This arrangement replaces the single concave shell that appeared on Queen Anne chests. Volutes also incorporated curved petals.

The unique combination of blocked form highlighted with shells is a stylistic arrangement that has never been surpassed in American furniture design.

These shells were more rhythmic and opulent than those of the previous era. When compared to the naturalistically carved shells used in Philadelphia, however, they continued to be highly stylized.

Another Newport case piece that successfully used the blocked form was the kneehole chest of drawers, a particular version of which was called a "bureau table." The kneehole form exists on English examples but it was rarely employed in the colonies outside of Rhode Island. The kneehole desk was so named for the cut out center of a dressing table that accommodates the sitter's legs.

Like the great majority of Newport pieces, the kneehole chest was made from mahogany and its design closely resembles the bottom of a Newport bookcase with a cut out in the middle. Fancy brasses and beading around the drawers provide horizontal emphasis and offset the vertical thrust of the blocked panels.

One of the most impressive pieces of eighteenth-century furniture ever conceived, the Rhode Island desk and bookcase turned out by the Goddard-Townsend School retained late Baroque undertones while advancing the blocked or "sweld" facade.

OPPOSITE PAGE: *Signed "John Cogswell, Middle Street, Boston, 1782," this mahogany chest-on-chest stands on a bombé or kettle-shaped base, a curvilinear form peculiar to Boston case furniture of the late eighteenth century.*

Courtesy The Museum of Fine Arts, Boston, MA, gift of Mr. and Mrs. Maxim Karolik

Blocked facades with carved shells appeared in various forms in neighboring states as well. Connecticut makers showed a particular interest in these surface configurations. Job Townsend might have introduced the technique to the area—he is believed to have spent time in Connecticut.

At first glance, a similarly blocked desk with shell motif is hard to distinguish from the Newport example from which it received its inspiration. On closer examination, the blocking on a similarly styled Connecticut case lacks the extreme tightness and optical tension between the vertical blocks and horizontal drawers that hallmarks the Newport chest.

Brasses are integral to a Newport chest; they set up six rectangles within horizontal tiers of drawers. They also separate the concave shell from its two adjacent convex shells. Connecticut brasses tend to be of the less ornate bail shape, and they do little more than perform a utilitarian function.

Cherry, the wood associated with Connecticut furniture, is less rich than mahogany. The eye tends to sit on the opaque surface instead of penetrating it. Shells, like the blocked panels they top, are looser and flatter. Connecticut cabinetmakers sometimes felt the need for additional ornament, possibly gadrooning, along the skirt, or large-scale scrolls separate from the bracket feet that try to recall those of Newport.

The eye can easily be trained to distinguish such subtleties, and it is up to the viewer to decide which rendition is the most appealing. One version can be appreciated for design integration while the other juxtaposes different design components to produce a specimen with character.

Along with bombé, oxbow, and serpentine shapes, Massachusetts cabinetmakers continued to use blocking in their case furniture. The form, which originated in Boston, was usually applied to chests with four drawers that span the width of the case.

Another Boston feature is a top and base viewed in plan, which follow the blocking of the carcass. Boston cabinetmakers limited blocking to the bottoms of large case pieces.

Some suggest that blocking on chests of drawers was originally conceived as a way to provide space for the knees of the sitter. The last edition of Chippendale's *Director* shows concave centers for "buroe dressing tables." Inaccuracies of perspective in these sketches may have eventually led to the flattening of this space when translated into actual pieces.

The block-front furniture of Boston, Newport, and Connecticut is well known. Portsmouth cabinetmakers, however, while less known than their Boston contemporaries, also produced cabinet pieces with blocked facades.

What separates Portsmouth blocking from that of other regions is its flat, rectilinear shape. The blocking is sharp at the corners, and somewhat flat in profile. These cases also stand on broader feet.

The Society for the Preservation of New England Antiquities counts among its collections two examples of Portsmouth block-front furniture. Scholarship on Portsmouth furniture has intensified recently and will hopefully yield insight into these pieces as well as into some other finely crafted Portsmouth forms that have yet to be attributed to a specific cabinetmaker.

Other case shapes that coexisted with the block-front form that were popularized in the last half of the eighteenth century include the oxbow front and the serpentine front. The serpentine facade moves in, out, and in across the surface; the oxbow reverses the serpentine curve to move out, in, and then out. The oxbow is alternately referred to as a reverse serpentine facade and is more typical of English work.

New England turned out the greatest number of serpentine chests in the colonies. A mahogany serpentine chest of drawers dated between 1760 to 1790 and now at the Museum of Fine Arts in Boston shares certain stylistic traits with a chest signed and dated by John Cogswell (1738–1818). The sturdy chest stands on squat cabriole legs and claw-and-ball feet. The fretwork that adorns the chamfered corners is a whimsical cross between Gothic and Chinese.

Certain clues below the base molding often help to pinpoint a specific shop. In this case, the stubby cabriole legs and the carving of the knees and articulated talons mimic those found on the Cogswell chest.

Jonathan Gostelowe (1744–1795) is recognized as one of Philadelphia's preeminent cabinetmakers. He assembled beautifully sculpted serpentine chests. Some characteristics that are credited to him include extremely large polygonal ogee bracket feet, ample use of bracing with glue blocks on drawer bottoms, simple bails, and cock beaded edges. Supplemental ornament consists of fretwork on the cantered corners.

Surprisingly, the Goddard–Townsend group produced a chest of drawers so Continental in shape that it renders absurd the contention that all Newport case furniture adheres to retardataire Baroque form.

This chest aspired to the modern French taste in form, but not in ornament. On loan to Boston's Museum of Fine Arts, this chest avoids the straight line in any plane, the standard by which any Rococo design is measured. It has been described as a "French message conveyed with a strong Yankee accent."

Probably made about 1770, this mahogany chest looks to the French commode for its validation. Peter Simon, a French sea captain, commissioned the piece, which may account for its pseudo-French form.

Its sweeping facade is accentuated with the flat urn brasses that adorn so many Chippendale chests. This chest is important for reasons beyond the obvious. Its existence proves that Newport artisans were certainly capable of expressing a stronger Rococo statement. They simply chose not to indulge it.

A Connecticut version working with the same serpentine vocabulary was less sophisticated. The reverse serpentine curve characteristic of British work appears with frequency. Rope-twisted columns, however, conclusively point to a Connecticut origin.

Seating ❦

In case furniture the transition from the Queen Anne to the Chippendale style was predominantly a change of ornament. The change in chair styles, however, was more fundamental, as it incorporated changes in form as well as in ornament.

Seat frames became square, crest rails were bow-shaped with ears, and splats were pierced in a variety of patterns. With few exceptions, stiles straightened out again. Carving ranged from the simple application of shells to all over acanthus or foliate detail.

The cabriole leg with claw-and-ball foot prevailed. Rare variants included the hairy paw and the scrolled, or whorl, foot. The whorl foot and the square-sectioned Marlborough leg were highlighted in the *Director.*

Structurally, the Massachusetts chair often retained remnants of the older style, especially the use of the stretchers to connect the legs and the thin proportions. Interwoven with these items were Chippendale attributes. These include the pierced splat and the bow-shaped crest rail with blunt ears.

Moving gently away from the S-curve of the Queen Anne cabriole leg, knees took on a sharpened form. Claw-and-ball feet became more birdlike with long, raked back talons. In typical Massachusetts construction, the side and front seat rails are tenoned into the upper part of the front legs. The squared seat frame has triangular strengthening corner blocks of horizontal grain that are glued and nailed.

The over-upholstered seat was an option that increased the final cost of a chair since it required more of the costly filling and fabric. In the third edition of the *Director,* Chippendale stated: "The Seats look best when stuffed over the Rails, and have a Brass Border neatly chased; but are most commonly done with Brass Nails, in one or two Rows; and sometimes the Nails are done to imitate Fretwork."

The "owl's eye" splat was the foremost design for Massachusetts Chippendale chair backs and was based on English examples. The chair descended stylistically from one published by the English designer, Robert Manwaring, in 1765. The cross-eyed owl splat became the ubiquitous Boston-Salem chair back and the shape spread to Portsmouth and Maine. Along with the owl's eye splat, these chairs are recognized by thin rails and sides.

The diamond back splat on this New York chair, circa 1755 to 1765, was preferred in New York, as was the flat knee carving. The slight kick-back on the rear legs is another often-seen trait. **OPPOSITE PAGE:** *These chairs reveal the progression of the older Queen Anne style, as found on the chair with a solid splat and simple pad feet, to the Chippendale style with pierced splats and claw-and-ball feet. The second chair from the left imposes a Chippendale pierced splat on an essentially Queen Anne form with a hoop-shaped crest and compass seat.*

These chairs enjoyed a long run, made from about 1755 to the turn of the century. Lacking specific documentation, a combined Boston-Salem attribution is often necessary due to the migration of craftsmen between the two areas. By the third quarter of the eighteenth century, Salem blossomed into a wealthy town with purchasing power that matched that of Boston.

While templates provide clues as to the shop origin in splats, variations in other components such as the amount of carving, the leg design, and foot shape were decisions that were often worked out between the cabinetmaker and his patron. These choices were made in accord with fashionable taste tempered by the ever remindful purse strings.

Philadelphia chairs continued to use stump legs, a holdover from Queen Anne chairs. Crest rails, splats, and seats reflected the modernizing input of the Chippendale directive.

Changes in cabinetmaking technique followed changes in form. A new method of support—in the form of quarter round, vertically grained corner blocks—was placed inside the squared seat frame that replaced the compass or balloon seat of the past.

Side rail construction called for tenons that were mortised through the rear leg, becoming exposed through the back of the chair. Sinewy carved claw-and-ball feet were smoother at the knuckles than those on Massachusetts chairs. Vigorous and lifelike carving contrasts with flatter and stylized carving found on Massachusetts chairs.

With some exceptions, Philadelphia Chippendale chairs follow three basic types of splat design that can be infinitely arranged. One type of pierced splat is a baluster with scrolled strapwork.

This is the most composite design of the three. The upper scrolls move down from the crest rail and stop about one-third of the way down the splat. These scrolls are met by two curved straps that grow out of the three-part shoe on the bottom of the splat.

The center bar divides into these two straps about one-third of the way up from the bottom. At the point where the bottom straps split, two interlaced straps move up to meet the bottom of the crest rail. These two straps are pivotal to the splat's design; without them the splat would appear disjointed.

In the second splat design, usually derived from English examples, a vase or baluster form is created from a swelling at the shoe or the base of the splat. Unlike the first type, the straps flow in uninterrupted lines to meet the crest rail. Peripheral carving does not prohibit this movement.

The third pierced splat found on Philadelphia chairs resembles Gothic tracery, including the quatrefoil that rests within the confines of the straps that emanate from the shoe.

The most celebrated of Philadelphia chairs is a group of chairs from a set that might once have numbered thirteen. Each chair represents both the highest expression of

Chippendale design to be found in the colonies and the most diligent workmanship.

Winterthur is home to one chair of this elaborate group. The mahogany side chair with white cedar secondary wood was made between 1770 and 1772, probably by Thomas Affleck (1740-1795). The flowing and airy splat is classified as a "Ribband Back" in accord with Chippendale's illustrations.

Due to its high level of sophistication and to certain typically English features, such as the saddle seat with partial over-upholstery, it was originally assumed that this chair was of English manufacture, possibly assembled in Philadelphia. It certainly rivals the best of English work in the St. Martin's Lane style.

Several other factors led antiquarians to the English pedigree. The carving that completely covers the surface of the chair is rare in American work. The hairy paw feet are somewhat uncommon on colonial furniture, usually found only on the highest-style Philadelphia and Massachusetts furniture. Abundant carving and hairy paw feet are usually linked to English and Irish practice.

However, the English attribution was discarded when analysis of the white cedar secondary woods revealed them to be of American origin.

Cabinetmaker Thomas Affleck included the separate charges for carver: James Reynolds and the shop of Nicholas Bernard and Martin Jugiez, whose skills were at a level appropriate to have executed such rich, cascading carvings. To date, these chairs are the purest strain of the Rococo taste in the United States.

An interesting provenance lends another level of interest to these chairs. They were ordered between 1770 and 1772 by General John Cadwalader for his townhouse in Philadelphia. Cadwalader was a man whom George Washington called a military genius and whom John Adams described as a "Gentleman of large Fortune with a grand and elegant House and Furniture."

The noted American artist Charles Wilson Peale portrayed Cadwalader, his wife, and daughter in a portrait that today is in the collection of the Philadelphia Metropolitan Museum of Art. The daughter is seated on a carved table with hairy paw feet.

In the realm of eighteenth-century portraiture, attributes, or the objects that were incorporated into the picture, gave important clues as to the sitter's economic and social position. How fitting that Peale chose to paint the portrait with a table that has come to signify the epitome of Philadelphia Rococo elegance.

The Philadelphia Chippendale style spread eastward to New Jersey and south to Maryland. Chairs from these regions are, therefore, close relatives to Philadelphia models. Maryland cabinetmakers chose to simplify the underlying form while exaggerating other aspects.

In the beginning of the nineteenth century, Baltimore became one of the fastest growing cities in the nation, complete with its own furniture center. Prior to that point, it followed Philadelphia practice with some variety. Broad proportions; bold, flaring ears; and straight legs with H-shaped stretchers best describe Maryland chairs.

BELOW: *One from a set of chairs made for Drayton Hall in Charleston, this chair acknowledges familiarity with premier English design as illustrated by Chippendale.* **OPPOSITE PAGE, TOP:** *Scroll feet, more typical of French work, were an alternative to claw-and-ball feet. Rarely used on colonial* furniture, the shape found favor in Philadelphia. The pattern for this chair was taken from Plate XII of the 1754 edition of the Director. **OPPOSITE, BOTTOM:** *The fluid acanthus leaf and foliate carving on this Philadelphia side chair is attributed to the shop of Nicholas Bernard and Martin Jugiez, circa 1762 to 1783.*

In the South, chairs assumed a rectilinear appearance. Legs were usually straight and were connected by H-shaped stretchers. The cabriole leg and claw-and-ball foot were infrequently used. Slip seats were square.

In Virginia, the typical back was fashioned from flat stiles and was moderately flared. The splat was vertically ribbed in a slightly upward flaring design. These splats were comprised of four ribs, some models of which were connected by horizontal bars at mid-point.

The crest rail might be straight, gently curved, or in distinctively southern fashion, terminate in circular, tightly scrolled ears. These chairs resemble rural English hall chairs with plank seats.

Charleston chairs have softly modelled ears and generally flat stiles. Regional taste preferred the straight leg with stretcher, the appearance of which corresponds to English variants. Splat design was the most decorative ingredient, and sophisticated looped figure splats are repeatedly credited to Thomas Elfe.

As always happens in furniture, when traits are too narrowly defined or stereotyped, exceptions to the rule surely follow. A mahogany side chair from about 1760 to 1780 at Greenfield Village and the Henry Ford Museum in Dearborn, Michigan, is a case in point.

The chair was part of a set made for John Drayton's Drayton Hall outside Charleston, South Carolina. Like the Cadwalader chairs, this piece reveals a familiarity with premiere English design.

Updated scholarship of the woods once again revealed non-English origins. Probably made in Charleston, the chair utilizes high-relief foliate carving of the strongest Rococo variety. The form lacks the synchronized flow of the Cadwalader chairs. The complicated pierced splat, for example, was executed in a stop-and-go manner and the stiles lack a sense of flowing interplay with the total design.

These qualities, combined with a slight imbalance between solid and void, suggests a more provincial judgment process. Such considerations aside, the chair is an important document of advanced colonial craftsmanship in a region that overwhelmingly patronized British cabinet-makers.

New York chairs continued to follow precedents set by their Queen Anne antecedents, notably the broad proportions and occasional use of the compass seat, which by this time was outdated. New York showed less variety in leg options; most legs were cabriole in form with a boxy claw-and-ball terminus.

inspired such composition. New York shared with Philadelphia a taste for Gothic contrivance; New England shared these tastes but to a lesser degree.

Splats with carved tassels and pendant ruffles are another example of how enterprising cabinetmakers copied patterns, in this case from Plate 15 of the *Director,* and spiced them with their own artistic contribution to create a distinctly colonial flavor.

Newport followed the same tradition with chairs as it had in case furniture; it was slower and more selective about embracing the Chippendale decree. Chairs retained their stretchers and hoop-shaped backs, but mixed them with up-to-date Chippendale ears and pierced splats.

Newport chairs of this persuasion share a pervasive sense of flatness from the stretchers to the knee to the flat carving. Back legs are often square, as are the seats. Cabriole legs have the four flat sides indicative of the Newport style.

In contrast to the less progressive chair cited above, Newport consumers also expressed interest in a rectilinear chair with a pierced splat that was a stylistic about-face from the Baroque holdover. Reminiscent of the owl-eyed splat found on a Massachusetts chair, the Newport version surprisingly followed the Robert Manwaring prototype more strongly.

The owl's eye splat has eyes that are decidedly less crossed than those on neighboring Massachusetts chairs. The Newport eyes project downward, not at each other.

Based on the superb craftsmanship shown in the chair's cross-hatched crest, fine scrolls, and stop-fluted Marlborough legs, John Townsend usually gets credit for its construction. Carving is shallow and portends the Neoclassical flavor that developed after the Revolution.

Many of these chairs survive; they are made from mahogany and occasionally from walnut. Seats were over-upholstered or slipped into the frame. Beyond their remarkable craftsmanship, these chairs are notable for their clean silhouettes and the equilibrium found between solid and void.

As a point of connoisseurship, this wonderfully orchestrated form and balance can be best seen if the viewer squints while observing the chair. This technique is helpful in assessing any form, as it blurs decorative distractions and allows the underlying shape to dominate.

Connecticut chairs show a miscellany that belie the state's small size. Some chairs from Hartford, for example, imitate Philadelphia models. Recall from the discussion of case furniture that Eliphalet Chapin trained in Philadelphia.

Stop-fluted Marlborough legs and clean yet graceful lines identify this Rhode Island walnut chair with the Goddard-Townsend School of cabinetmakers. Its design was based on those by Englishman Robert Manwaring.

Many New York chairs have rear legs with a slight kick-back at the bottom. Seats were often highlighted with gadrooning or thickly fluted repetitive carving.

New York chairs parallel the English George II format, mainly in the broad measurements of the seats and knees. Whereas legs and feet in New York followed a singular format, splats showed greater creativity. One version was a pierced splat with a diamond meeting interlaced loops. Another pierced splat had a Gothic flavor. Imported English chairs and/or plates from Chippendale's *Director*

Upon his return to Connecticut, he consolidated numerous Philadelphia structural and decorative overlays.

Some of these overlays included through tenons, stump legs, interlaced scroll patterns, and shell-carved crest rails. Chapin mixed these with native Connecticut cherry and flared roll-back ears.

On easy chairs, some properties that signal regional taste include some of the same features that are noted on Queen Anne chairs: C-scrolled arm supports in Philadelphia, broad proportions and boldly flared wings in New York, and vertically rolled arms in New England. What differentiates Chippendale versions from those of earlier chairs is the amount and type of carving on the cabriole legs, which in many cases, matches that found on side- and armchairs.

Two especially attractive sofa forms were found in New York and in Philadelphia. A New York model had a deeply serpentined back and a curved front rail. An urbane model with double peaks in the serpentine back represented the best of Philadelphia design.

Chairs with owl-eyed splats and thin seats were standard fare in the Boston/Salem area. The pad feet were less costly alternatives to the claw-and-ball variety and were chosen by the patron.

Courtesy C.L. Prickett, Yardley, PA

Courtesy Leigh Keno, NYC

OPPOSITE PAGE: *The scalloped piecrust edge on this tilt-top table is one of the best of its kind.* **ABOVE:** *Perhaps the heartiest sculptural tea table ever made, this Boston mahogany table designed to hold fourteen cups avoids the straight line in any plane. The turreted apron sets up a positive and negative image and rests on cabriole legs.*

Several new types of tables joined the ranks of established forms such as the tea table, card table, side table, and drop-leaf table. The new forms, including small kettle stands with slide-out trays to hold teacups, continued to complement the genteel pursuits of the merchant class.

Some high points of table design include a turret-top tea table, which was highly prized in Boston. The Museum of Fine Arts in Boston contains the heartiest sculptural table of this type. The entire apron of the skirt is turreted, resulting in a positive and negative image. The turrets are evenly spaced to hold fourteen cups.

Adding to the complexity of the skirt is the shape of the top, which echoes the shape of the sides. Cabriole legs are quite "leggy" and end in choice claw-and-ball feet. Acanthus leaf carving is applied with a modicum of restraint to the knees. Made from mahogany and dated 1750 to 1775, it shows the same reverence for sculptural beauty as does much neighboring furniture from Newport.

A tea or silver table from Portsmouth, New Hampshire, could be quite *au courant* in its styling. One of the Diplomatic Reception Rooms at the Department of State in Washington, D.C., contains one of the approximately six extant examples based on Plate 34 of the *Director.*

The rectangular mahogany table has a pierced fret gallery that borders the top. Marlborough legs of the same lightness that typify much New Hampshire furniture are enhanced with decorative brackets where they meet the case. An unusual domed stretcher formed from double C-scrolls is topped with a spiral finial and is quite functional. The height and shape of the stretcher provide anyone standing at the table with adequate room for his or her feet.

This form was known in Philadelphia but it didn't reach the same level of refinement that it did in Portsmouth. Based on the level of workmanship, it is clear that skilled English cabinetmakers didn't settle only in one place.

As a rule, Newport craftsmen consciously steered away from too much dependence on Chippendale stricture. But the surfacing of one form, the Pembroke table, shows that copies of the *Director* were known in Newport.

The form, which charmed Rhode Island cabinetmakers and their sponsors, was based on an illustration from the *Director.* A variant of the drop-leaf table, the Pembroke was smaller in scale. Besides its smaller size, one easy way to distinguish a Pembroke table is by the leaves; Pembroke tables reverse the proportions of a drop-leaf. The center section is usually wider than the drop-leaves.

Designed as a breakfast table, and used alternately for serving tea and small meals, it stands on four Marlborough legs, has two hinged leaves and a single drawer. The Pembroke table's compact size assured that it would be pressed into service frequently throughout the day.

One example bearing the label of John Townsend epitomizes Newport understatement. Chippendale's fancy Chinese fret for the apron is transformed into the pierced X-shaped stretcher that repeats dots and dashes. Townsend added his own enhancements, including stop-fluting on the legs and pierced brackets that connect the leg to the base.

Philadelphia Pembroke tables evoke Chippendale's designs more literally, with scalloped edges on the leaves as well as flat pierced stretchers.

Philadelphia originated the piecrust tilt-top table that is the standard by which all tilt-tops are judged. This form, along with the high chest, represents the pinnacle of Philadelphia Chippendale creativity.

The piecrust top has the scalloped edges that resemble the crust of a pie. It was designed to sit on top of a birdcage

New York cabinetmakers excelled in the five-legged card table. This boldly modelled example has gadrooning across the skirt and rather blocky claw-and-ball feet, both decorative subtleties attractive to New York consumers.

support made up of two blocks between the pedestal and the top separated by vertical columns. This device allows the top to tilt.

The column or pillar meets a tripod base that concludes with claw-and-ball feet that are flattened, earning them the nickname of "rat claws." Ideas about what constitutes the best of the form include quality carving, nicely turned columns, and an overall integration strategy with the tripod base.

As Philadelphia excelled in the piecrust tilt-top table, New York excelled in the card table. This boldly modelled piece compensates for the paucity of sculptural form in much New York Chippendale case furniture.

These tables are identified by a sturdy overall appearance softened by serpentine curves on the sides and top. Blunt corners make a sharp contrast to the undulating lines of the carcass. Massachusetts and Pennsylvania examples, by contrast, have turreted corners.

The unique fifth leg that swings to support the top in an open position is peculiar to New York. Gadrooning, or swirled fluting across the skirt, was another decorative frill that appealed to the New York market.

Hearty cabriole legs with claw-and-ball feet were standard fare on a mahogany veneer on beech body. Lavish acanthus and C-scroll carving supplemented with cross-hatching found its best expression on the knees. The approximately twenty-five surviving examples of this form are considered the classic and definitive New York Chippendale statement.

The other form that was linked to New York is the spider-leg table. Fashioned after a popular English design, this delicate table is the antithesis of the sculptural five-legged game table.

Visually, it is a throwback to the gate-leg tables of decades past, although its lightness certainly points to a late eighteenth-century date of construction.

With a square mahogany top, it stands on painfully thin turned legs that are reinforced with equally thin stretchers. John Singleton Copley, the premier colonial portraitist of the eighteenth century, captured the form for posterity in his 1774 portrait, *Mr. and Mrs. Isaac Winslow.* Copley painted the hands of his subjects with a lightness and curvature that matches the delicacy and curved apron of the table upon which they rest.

Bedsteads

Chippendale bedsteads were predominantly the high-post type with curtains and a tester. The bedding, or soft goods, continued to be the most expensive component. Posts varied from those that were turned and carved to models with fluting. Less frequently found are low-post bedsteads with a serpentine headboard and deception beds in which the sleeping surface is hidden in a case that resembles a chest of drawers.

Stop fluting has been found on Newport examples, and less frequently, on New York and Connecticut designs. Legs terminate in blocked or claw-and-ball feet, and some New York bedsteads have carved footposts.

Courtesy The Henry Francis du Pont Winterthur Museum, DE

A high-post bedstead draped in expensive fabric was a luxury found in the most upscale households. This model is from Philadelphia circa 1780 to 1790.

Part II ✦ Neoclassical Furniture
(1790–1840)

The Federal Style (1790–1815)

The Empire Style (1815–1840)

The Restauration, or Pillar and Scroll, Style
(1830–1840)

With the Revolution ended, and America in its political infancy, economic independence became a primary goal. Foreign trade was the method by which America was to achieve economic success, and it proved to be the route to great wealth for many individual entrepreneurs. One such risk-taker was Elias Hasket Derby, one of America's first millionaires, whose wealth contributed to the growth of American furniture making.

Wherever ambition and their ships would carry them, American shipping entrepreneurs went, including such faraway destinations as South America, the Pacific, and China. By the last decade of the eighteenth century, the China trade accounted for an increasingly large percentage of imports to America. Porcelain, a staple of American trade with China, often served as ballast for ships returning laden with the luxuries of the Far East. Its importation helped satisfy a strong demand that would, with several exceptions, go unmet by American artisans for several decades. George and Martha Washington led a long list of American aesthetes who commissioned porcelain services. On the domestic scene, the American population numbered approximately four million and was scattered across a wider geographic area. And while shipping and trade made fortunes for many enterprising individuals, most Americans still derived their livelihood from farming.

The Revolution granted the colonies political and economic independence, but in matters of material culture, America still turned to England both for her wares, necessities, and luxuries, and for trends in furniture design. One sector of the population with demands held over from the lean days of the Revolution saw nothing reprehensible about securing ideas and goods from England. Others felt differently.

Along with Noah Webster, who admonished Americans to become more inwardly directed in the arts, were others who warned that "madness of foreign finery rages and destroys, threatening convulsions and dissolution to the political body."

Nevertheless, it was to England, and for the first time, to France, that American furniture makers looked for the designs that would rule the nineteenth century. A dramatic shift in American furniture occurred at this time, prompted by changes that had been taking place in English and French furniture design dating back to the late 1760s. The main ingredient in this stylistic shift was a resurgence of classicism. This trend gained momentum with the dis-covery of items of classical antiquity in late eighteenth-century archaeological digs at Herculaneum and through the unearthing of the wondrous ruins at Pompeii. The western world's love affair with classicism came to be known as Neoclassicism.

In the body of American stylistic development, the Neoclassical influence progressed somewhat systematically through three phases. The Federal style (1790–1815) was marked by the application of classical motifs to contemporary furniture forms. The Empire style (1815–1840) aimed for greater archaeological accuracy in form and in ornament. The last phase, the Restauration, or Pillar and Scroll, style (1830–1840) reduced forms to simple "pillar and scroll" shapes that made use of developing technology. These three periods defined Neoclassicism in America.

As the new nation achieved economic success, prosperity increased Americans' demands for luxurious living. An influx of skilled English craftsmen met this demand and simultaneously assured a product astoundingly similar to that made by English sources.

At the same time, the character of the nation was changing, and individual regions developed their own identities. Philadelphia reached its social and economic peak. It was a city admired for its elegance and a sophistication that rivalled that of London.

The construction of the Lancaster Pike in the 1790s made the city the gateway to the West and created road systems that allowed land travel to compete with water travel for the first time. As a center of the new nation's banking system, the city received added prestige.

Sophisticated Philadelphians eagerly adopted the Neoclassical style as depicted in the latest series of imported English pattern books by George Hepplewhite and Thomas Sheraton. A French influence can be noted in the highly developed tastes of individuals such as John Adams, Thomas Jefferson, and James Monroe, all of whom lived in Philadelphia when the city was the nation's capital.

Baltimore came to be known as "one of the fairest cities of North America, in point of wealth and trade, occupying the first place after Philadelphia, New York, and Boston." Its port controlled shipping on the Chesapeake Bay, and the city became the gateway to the South.

By the late 1790s, New York had surpassed its rival cities of Boston and Philadelphia in foreign trade. The commercial activities that dominated New York City were carried out by merchants, shipping brokers, and insurance agents. The New York Stock Exchange was founded during this peak of activity. New York's prosperity enhanced its cosmopolitan social life, which gained an extra cachet during the city's year-long position as the nation's capital.

As in Philadelphia, sophisticated patrons in New York demonstrated a taste for French objects and were receptive to French émigré craftsmen who brought early nineteenth-century styles with them. But in keeping with the diversity of its underlying population, New York pieces also embodied the best of English form and ornament.

This was most apparent in the work of Duncan Phyfe, who has been credited with some of the greatest cabinet-making skills in the history of American furniture. Phyfe's aggressive sales and marketing organization further ensured the widespread appreciation of his work.

Boston remained the hub of New England, and by the late eighteenth century the moral imperatives of Puritanism had receded somewhat. In the early nineteenth century, the town of Salem, courtesy of the China trade, rivalled Boston in purchasing power.

The Massachusetts shipping magnate, Elias Hasket Derby, kept artisans from Salem to Philadelphia busy furnishing his house as well as those of his family. Puritan sumptuary laws had little effect on the architecture or furnishing of the grand houses of Salem, residences and pieces that today remain as synonyms of Federal design and exemplify the riches the China trade afforded Yankee merchants.

The War of 1812 interrupted the flow of trade across the Atlantic, but in 1815 the nation resumed those commercial activities that had suffered during the war and blockade. International shipping picked up, carrying American goods to ports where they could be exchanged for products suitable for the American marketplace.

New towns sprouted out of the great expanse of the West. Cleveland and Cincinnati were two such cities. Westward expansion placed increasing demands on the nation's fledgling communications network.

In the words of John Calhoun, "We are great, and rapidly—I was about to say fearfully—growing... This is our pride and our danger; our weakness and our strength... Let us, then, bind the republic together with a perfect system of roads and canals."

The stirring of technology made Calhoun's visions possible. A system of thoroughfares, including the National Road, was constructed to connect the nation. The Erie Canal project hastened waterway travel. Robert Fulton's steamboats were a unique combination of grandeur and efficiency. In certain river towns they were in abundance.

In the decorative arts, America entered the second phase of Neoclassicism, or the Empire. The style, from 1815 to 1840, was well suited to the tenacity of the new nation.

America embarked on its own course of Empire. The Society of the Cincinnati, made up of officers of the Continental Army, was a patriotic organization formed at the end of the eighteenth century. Its name was borrowed from the Roman general Cincinnatus. Cincinnatus returned victorious from war to resume more pastoral pursuits. Washington and his troops set out on a similar course to build anew after the Revolution and the War of 1812.

Benjamin Henry Latrobe, the British-trained architect, came to America at the end of the eighteenth century. He is best remembered for overseeing the completion of the White House after its near-demise by British forces.

By 1830, America's landscape was cluttered with classical structures that quoted Greek principles. They met Latrobe's expectations that "the days of Greece may be revived in the woods of America." Ever pragmatic American craftsmen relied on clapboard painted white to recall the marble palaces of antiquity. Marble itself was used much more judiciously.

A unique consistency can be found in the architecture and furniture of America's Neoclassical era. The strong architecture-decorative arts link became an American phenomenon, as elements of style were readily exchanged between the two disciplines.

In the decade between 1830 and 1840, the population continued its rapid growth and westward thrust, numbering more than seven million people. By this time, democratic ideals were firmly rooted. The quest for material possessions and comfort was foremost in the minds of the general population. At the same time, American life was becoming increasingly complex.

Advances in technology made it a double-edged sword, for as mechanization began to increase production efficiency, it did so at the expense of the artisan. Art became separate from industry. The individual creative efforts that had once fostered originality of design gave way to mechanized processes that could produce a piece faster and less expensively, even if they sacrificed elements of style.

By the mid-nineteenth century, the cabinetmaker's status in the labor force had plummeted. The craftsman's eyes and hands, once valued for their ability to perceive, interpret, and create unique designs, were increasingly replaced by the skills of the itinerant worker necessary to the repetitive assembly process that came to define the furniture industry. It is at this point that the discussion of customized American furniture-making ends.

Federal Style
(1790–1815)

America must be "as famous for arts as for arms."

Noah Webster

Moving away from a solipsistic colonial mindset, America took off in new directions, literally and figuratively. The economy was rebounding from the effects of the American Revolution, and westward expansion with its ancillary doctrine of "manifest destiny" had begun. The Louisiana Purchase of 1803 was the summation of these activities.

Paradoxically, to look back in history was to look ahead, and patriotic, socially minded visionaries such as Thomas Jefferson connected philosophically with the great civilizations of Greece and Rome in formulating the "promise of America."

As representative government deposed the centuries-old paradigm of the divine right of kings, the rediscovery of Herculaneum and Pompeii prompted the inescapable

rebellion against the curved line. Neoclassicism was introduced to America shortly after the Revolution. Use of the term "Federal" coincides with the formation of the new nation and its central or federal government. Federal furniture thus became the iconology of America's evolution from a colonial dominion to that of an autonomous nation.

During this period, in contrast to the era of colonial furniture, where trans-Atlantic transmission of style was courtesy of the British Isles, France would come to play a more direct role than it had in the past. And while elements were merging from various world style centers to form the Neoclassical vocabulary, it was the Scottish architect and designer, Robert Adam, who had the profoundest influence on early Neoclassicism.

Style Overview

After a four-year period of study in Italy, Adam returned to the United Kingdom with a classical vocabulary that would signal the death knoll of the Rococo in England. He believed strongly in the design credo that held that a building's interiors should reflect its exterior, for a coherent design theme.

In 1761, Adam designed the dining room at Kedleston, an English country estate at Derbyshire, in England. It showcased a unified approach to interior decoration. The room was conceived with such classical accoutrements as inset symmetrical ornament, paintings, and plasterwork of palmettes, sphinxes, and acanthus. The room was broken into squares, rectangles, circles, and ovals.

Throughout his work, Adam stressed the interrelation of a room's parts through a unifying decorative scheme. Floor coverings echoed ceiling design; even minute details such as handles and escutcheons on doors came under the classical scrutiny of the architect. Originally geared specifically to an upscale market, Adam's strict message was codified and disseminated to a wider, middle-class market by a host of pattern books.

The most famous pattern books to promulgate Adam's Neoclassical ideal to Federal cabinetmakers were George Hepplewhite's *The Cabinetmaker and Upholsterer's Guide* of 1788 and Thomas Sheraton's *The Cabinet-Maker and Upholsterer's Drawing Book* (1791–1794).

What Chippendale's *Director* was to the Rococo, Hepplewhite's *Guide* and Sheraton's *Drawing Book* were to the Federal style. Antiquarians occasionally refer to pieces as being in the Hepplewhite or in the Sheraton manner.

Loosely described, Hepplewhite's sketches depict furniture with straight, tapered legs and spade feet, or on case pieces, flared bracket feet. Chairs were fashioned with curvilinear shield, oval, or heart-shaped backs.

LEFT: *A series of geometrically amassed components, this Federal secretary generates appeal with simple outlines, veneered and inlaid surfaces, and drawer pulls of restrained design.*
RIGHT: *The penultimate tribute to its maker, Aaron Willard of Massachusetts, this Federal clock juxtaposes the strength of a gilded eagle with the delicacy of the gilt foliate ornament. It is a high point of Neoclassical design.*

LEFT: *The carved basket of fruit and snowflake-punched background are hallmarks of Samuel McIntire of Salem, Massachusetts.* **BELOW LEFT:** *Typical of McIntire's finesse, this Federal chair has a back with a Gothic flavor, the original design of which appeared in Hepplewhite's* Guide.

These designs were less ornate than the designs suggested by Adam. All pieces were based on the classical imperative of symmetry. Hepplewhite often favored light wood stringing, marquetry, or inlay on dark grounds.

Thomas Sheraton's *Drawing Book* went a long way toward popularizing the rectangular shape. Square-back seating predominated; legs followed those of Hepplewhite's chairs, with reeding, a novelty that became especially important to nineteenth-century design.

Decorative reeding is a series of vertical lines that are convex. This contrasts with the fluting found on eighteenth-century furniture that relies on multiple vertical concave lines. Many Sheraton pieces are recognized by color fields with contrasting light and dark woods.

These descriptions serve only as an approximation. Select pieces on occasion contain principles of either style; Hepplewhite and Sheraton occasionally exchanged each other's elements.

Due to overlaps in time and in treatment, it is best to describe early nineteenth-century American furniture within the larger scope of Neoclassicism or the Federal style. Characteristics that best allude to the Federal style include fineness of scale, dissolved at times to the point of excessive leanness.

Other hallmarks include classical symmetry and heavy reliance on geometric shapes, including the square, circle, and oval. These elements were executed by a hand tempered with a delicacy unknown in the past. The stranglehold that architecture had over case pieces lessened substantially. Case pieces became a combination of geometric parts, while chairs and small tables displayed their thinness.

In another about face from Rococo ornament, Federal carving often focused on the surface rather than projecting from it as it had, for example, on Philadelphia furniture of the previous era. Those familiar with early Neoclassical silver might see a similarity between the shallow engraving on those pieces and the low-relief carving on furniture of the same time. All decorative arts tended to follow this general trend toward flatness.

Motifs alluded to the days of Rome: Swags, ribbons, urns, paterae (round or oval forms with radiating patterns), and Prince of Wales feathers were common. All motifs were applied in a balanced and/or repetitive arrangement.

Mahogany furniture continued to be made but there was a general shift toward light-colored woods such as satinwood, beech, and bird's eye maple. These woods provided the contrast of light against dark that was a critical component of Federal avant-garde taste.

Ebony, selectively placed, exaggerated details such as spade feet. Rosewood, another alternative to mahogany, became more popular as the century progressed.

Much Federal furniture derives its visual importance and charm from the use of inlay. The inlay process creates designs flush with the surface by mixing grains, color, texture, or other non-wood materials. The technique varies from applying patterns to solid wood to assembling small pieces of veneer and affixing them to a backing.

The distinct shape the inlay takes can be divided into categories. It is called stringing if it is a narrow band of inlay such as that found around drawers. Wood mosaics that form geometric patterns are called parquetry; marquetry, on the other hand, is more pictorial. It incorporates flowers, shells, and other non-linear shapes.

This trio of inlays, combined with brilliantly figured and matched veneers, supplanted carving as the primary component of applied Federal ornament. As is the case with all American furniture to this point, each geographic region expressed a preference for a distinct inlay pattern.

A word of caution about inlay patterns. Since the technique was so popular and was so widely used, firms specialized in its manufacture both here and abroad. Many patterns were imported. So while inlay can be a clue to regional American origin, it should not be the only determining factor in attribution.

Inlay reached a level of artistic expression in the Federal period that has yet to be equalled in furniture of American lineage. Much of the exactness of the patterns is lost in photographs. For purposes of connoisseurship, it is

A visual treasure chest of Federal cabinetmaking, this mahogany and satinwood desk and bookcase by John Davey and John Davey, Jr. under- *scores the Philadelphia preference for large areas of contrasting veneer. It is geometry in wood.*

Carving on Federal furniture differed markedly from the flowing, naturalistic style of Rococo composition. Federal carving is less sculptural, less ornate, and less encompassing.

The compact tambour desk was a new form in the Federal period. It was a specialty of Massachusetts cabinetmakers, and the Seymour firm turned out the best examples, with fine inlay of contrasting light and dark veneers.

important to view actual pieces to understand the beauty and complexity of the process.

Veneering, inlay, and shallow or bas-relief carving were rarely challenged by other decorative embellishments. Painted surfaces, however, did win favor among elite buyers on a limited basis in Boston and on a larger scale in Baltimore.

Drawer pulls, escutcheon plates, and other hardware were subjugated to their utilitarian roles. Unlike their Chippendale and Queen Anne counterparts, they rely less on free-form design. Discreet Federal brasses used simple geometric shapes that reflected the mathematical precision of the pieces to which they were attached. Oval brasses with bails or rosettes with rings were among the most favored shapes.

Despite the new political unity in America, in furniture design regionalism continued. The reasons for its persistence are as diverse as the furniture itself.

The makeup of the population continued to reflect a diversity in ethnic background. Immigrants from England, Scotland, and Ireland joined those from the Continent in forming broad-based patterns of consumption. In addition, Federal America was not dominated by a single style center such as London or Paris. Instead, different regions possessed their own centers, and consumers were confronted with a smorgasbord of choices.

After recovering from the effects of the Revolution, cabinetmaking shops for the first time began to build stock or inventory to complement custom work. It is probable that inventory building encouraged a certain amount of repetitiveness and thereby fostered regional practice.

New England patrons remained largely reserved in their taste. There, the new Federal forms peacefully coexisted at times with older styles in the same room. Federal furniture produced in New England was known for its elegance and fineness of scale. Of the many talented artists servicing this clientele in the Boston-Salem area, John Seymour (1738–1818), his son, Thomas (1771–1848), and Samuel McIntire (1757–1811) produced some of the best crafted, most innovative, and aesthetically pleasing forms of the Federal period.

Samuel McIntire was the woodcarver and architect who designed the Pierce-Nichols house in Salem. He started out as a carver of figureheads for ships before turning to furniture. McIntire is well known for his distinctive carving style, which often features a basket of fruit. The Seymours were a cabinetmaking dynasty not unlike the Goddards and Townsends of Newport. John was trained in England before emigrating to America, where he and his son Thomas operated a large workshop in Boston. The Seymours were known for their particularly fine inlay work.

The New England region that changed most during the Federal period was Newport. The Goddard sons, Stephen and Thomas, carried on the cabinetmaking legacy of their father, John, but the town ultimately lost its leadership position.

Furniture made from cherry with elaborate inlays made up of wavy lines arranged as pinwheels point to a Connecticut origin. Eliphalet Chapin in East Windsor and his son

Aaron in Hartford continued to turn out furniture of the highest quality, the latter in the Hepplewhite style.

During the Federal period, New York became a center of urban life. Its status was elevated economically through foreign trade; its tonnage eschewed that of its rival ports, Boston and Philadelphia. New York City drew immigrants of considerable diversity. The Scotsman, Duncan Phyfe (1768–1854), came to New York in the late eighteenth century and through a combination of skill and business acumen, came to dominate New York furniture making, leaving a legacy of furniture that has stood the test of time. His name is indelibly linked with the New York Neoclassical perspective.

A French émigré, Charles-Honoré Lannuier (1779–1819), arrived in New York in the 1790s, bringing with him the French Directoire style, named for the group of five leaders who governed France immediately following the Reign of Terror. The Directoire approach was a more moderate interpretation of the grandiose Louis XVI style. As France rejected its king, so the Directoire style disavowed the ornate.

Lannuier quickly established his shop, endearing himself to an expanding New York audience. Like Phyfe, he later embraced archaeological classicism in the next stage of American Neoclassicism, the Empire.

In Philadelphia, once the bastion of Chippendale-Rococo fantasy, forms took on precisely geometric linear shapes. Broad, plain veneers with large color field differences were often paired with stringing inlay.

The French influence in America was strongest in Philadelphia. French furniture was imported to satisfy the francophiles, Gouverneur Maurice (1752–1816) among them. He purchased a set of furniture from Versailles. Philadelphia was the only Federal city to entertain the Louis XVI style to any perceptible degree. Two master cabinetmakers from Philadelphia include Henry Connelly (1770–1826) and Ephraim Haines (1755–1837).

The American Revolution was a watershed for Baltimore, marking not only the achievement of political freedom but also of artistic freedom. For the first time, Baltimore became an important center for independent furniture design. Prior to the Revolution the city's cabinetmakers labored under the creative auspices of Philadelphia.

Of all Federal furniture, that from Baltimore shows the strongest affinity for English Neoclassical work. Baltimore did not express the strong penchant for French taste that Philadelphia did.

Characteristic designs were based on sketches laid out by Sheraton. A famous group of ladies' cabinet or secretary desks closely allude to English precedents.

Another characteristic that denotes a Baltimore origin is the technique of *verre églomisé,* or reverse painting or gilding on glass panels. It is usually pictorial in nature.

A distinct category of Baltimore pieces that captured the imagination was painted, or "fancy," furniture. The painted furniture differed significantly from the light, floral-based versions that were popular in Boston at the beginning of the nineteenth century. Baltimore painted

Pictured is a flame birch-veneered and inlaid mahogany chest with a bowed front from Portsmouth, New Hampshire, circa 1790 to 1810. The series of rectangles formed by the contrasting panels reaffirms the case's geometric precision.

Small work tables were designed to hold fabric and sewing implements and they became increasingly popular as women displayed "fancy" silk needlework, including samplers. This example was made in Boston.

pieces were the nineteenth-century equivalents of japanned furniture.

Baltimore painted creations were an eclectic grouping of landscapes, flora, and bows, all rendered with polychrome paint. Brothers John and Hugh Finlay, Irish born and trained, are linked with this highly decorative interpretation of a London fad.

Baltimore cabinetmakers also relied heavily on inlay. The most recognizable pattern is the bellflower inlay with an elongated central petal.

In the pre-Revolutionary years, Charleston's furniture crafters produced a thoroughly English-inspired product that reflected its strong link to English material culture.

After the Revolution, Charleston continued this precedent with one notable addition. Shipping records show that Charleston increasingly imported domestically made furniture from Philadelphia and New York. Some Charleston furniture, especially the shield-back side chairs, so closely resemble New York examples that the onus falls heavily on provenance and secondary woods in determining a place of origin.

Charleston also shared some inlay patterns with New York. The Charleston area, though, wasn't without its own distinctive motif. Some pieces wear a distinctive rice pattern, this unusual motif paying homage to one of the heartiest of southern crops.

Case Pieces

As if to signal the end of the colonial era, the reign of the high chest as the definitive case piece came to an end. The form was replaced with the chest-on-chest or double chest of drawers that first appeared in quantity during the Chippendale years.

Perhaps the most renowned chest-on-chests were a group of four that were commissioned by Elias Hasket Derby of Salem, Massachusetts. His Salem home, designed by Samuel McIntire, was described as "more like a palace than the dwelling of an American merchant."

Shortly after the home's completion, both Derby and his wife died. In the resulting squabbling over the vast fortune, the house was demolished and its contents distributed among the heirs. Extant furniture from this dwelling provides important clues to style and taste in one of America's wealthiest nineteenth-century families.

One of the Derby chest-on-chests is now in Boston at the Museum of Fine Arts. Its form is somewhat retarded, being reminiscent of Chippendale chests with bracket feet, but its ornament is unmistakably Federal. The mahogany chest was assembled in Salem by William Lemon and decorated by Samuel McIntire. The large chest had a serpentine bottom, columns, and an architectural pediment topped with two large urns and an allegorical female figure.

Telltale McIntire traits include the carved cornucopia, basket of fruit, and the snowflake punchwork that appears as a background device on the bracket feet. Lion's head pulls and tiny stringing around the drawers reaffirm the chest's Neoclassical orientation.

The chest was made for Derby's daughter, Elizabeth, in 1796. In an invoice dated that same year, McIntire billed Elizabeth directly for the carving.

From the Seymour shop came a demilune commode. In 1809, Thomas Seymour billed Derby's daughter, Elizabeth, eighty dollars for a "Large Mahogany Commode"

Made in 1809 by Thomas Seymour for the Derby family of Salem, this European-inspired demilune commode reflects a high-style Massachusetts aesthetic that included the lunette of painted shells rendered on top by John Ritto Penniman.

OPPOSITE PAGE: *One of four chest-on-chests commissioned by Elias Hasket Derby of Salem, this mahogany chest made by William Lemon has the serpentine bottom and ogee bracket feet suggestive of Chippendale work but the ornament is unmistakably Federal. The carving was done by Samuel McIntire.*

inspired form is part of a small but elite group of painted Boston furniture.

The body of the commode was fashioned from mahogany, mahogany veneer, and maple and satinwood veneers. Radiating out of the lunette of painted shells are alternating bands of light and dark inlay. Carved mahogany columns encase three sections of graduated four-tier drawers; the columns were possibly carved by Thomas Whitman.

The brass animal paw feet and imported lion's head pulls reflect the attention to detail inherent in a piece of this magnitude. Along with other objects from the Derby family, this commode reflects the zenith of the Federal idiom.

A diminutive secretary and bookcase with a simplicity of design that merged the features of a bookcase and cabinet is often referred to in the trade as a "Salem secretary." The scale of these pieces suggests that they were probably made for women.

Like so much other case furniture that spanned these years, the Salem secretary was comprised of simple linear shapes. A box-like top with glass doors decked with curtains rested on an equally square base. The top was finished with an extremely flat, almost horizontal pediment and simple finials.

The bottom case houses a secretary drawer, an innovation of the Federal period. This allows the writing surface to fold up vertically so that the space resembles the drawers over which it sits. The secretary drawer replaces the slant-top configurations of the past.

Legs on a model at the Museum of Fine Arts in Boston have simple splayed bracket feet suggestive of Hepplewhite designs. Simple in outline, what gives the piece such appeal is a handsome matched veneered surface that is accented with simple brasses.

Somewhat larger in scale was the gentleman's secretary. It was the preferred form in northeastern New England. With the same geometric shape as the Salem secretary, the top was usually made up of four glass cabinets (versus the two on a Salem secretary) whose patterns were another geometric shape—triangles, half circles, and permutations of the two.

Small pediments with tightly restrained urns or balls stand in marked contrast to the large scrolled tops and open flame finials of earlier colonial models. The bottom half was another series of boxes with the center section housing the writing compartment.

The adjacent cabinets provided storage, and the surface of these bases was arranged in an infinite variety of contrasting geometric forms superimposed on each other;

and an extra ten dollars because he "Paid Mr. Penniman's Bill, for Painting Shels on Top of D°." John Ritto Penniman (1783–1837) was a Boston artist; the bill relates to the decorative shell painting that he rendered in the lunette on the top of the case.

The high quality of the brushwork is as technically masterful as that found in still life paintings. This European-

they are geometry in wood. Light and dark veneers provide contrast.

The secretaries stand on short, thin turned legs that sometimes terminate in spade feet. Sheraton summarized the secretary best when he commented: "This piece is intended for a gentleman to write at, to keep his own accounts, and serves as a library. The stage of finishing is neat, and sometimes approaching to elegance." Some examples are lifted from his *Dictionary.*

The sense of movement that had been so prevalent in eighteenth-century furniture dissolved, as the use of stringing and banding held the eye within the confines of the geometric proportions. As the Chippendale piece shouted aspiration, the Federal piece whispered affirmation.

Philadelphia cabinetmakers turned out secretary-bookcases with more vertical emphasis than did their peers in Massachusetts. An example at the Metropolitan Museum of Art in New York made by John Davey and John Davey, Jr. (a. 1797–1822) underscores this tendency.

Severely geometric in form, the two-part case is divided visually into six inlaid ovals that are further set into squares and rectangles that blur the distinction between top and bottom. In an abstract way, flame mahogany provides depth to an otherwise flat body.

A flat cornice with a small rounded panel in the center sits with dignity on top. Horizontal bands of satinwood work to balance the vertical bias. Two satinwood panels are inset with oval glass.

The bottom case is a series of light and dark veneers that illustrates the Philadelphia preference for large areas of contrasting veneers. This differentiates the piece from those of New England, where smaller color fields or plain mahogany-veneered surfaces were preferred.

Short outward splayed legs and simple curved skirt provide a hint of relief from the form's consistently straight lines. Pencilled in ten different places are the signatures of its makers. The Federal period saw an increase in signatures and labels that can be attributed in part to pride in workmanship.

The Baltimore secretary-bookcase was one of the most unique of Federal forms as well as one of the highest in style. Plate 38 of Sheraton's 1803 publication, *The Cabinet Dictionary,* was known as the "Sister's Cylinder Bookcase." It served as the inspiration for many Baltimore desks.

The form is H-shaped with two narrow cabinets forming the verticals. A rectangular writing compartment with drawers, pigeonholes, and drop-front writing surface substitutes for the cylindrical section of Sheraton's design.

The top of each pedestal houses a glass door that sits atop another cabinet. This cabinet, in turn, rests on an inverted pyramid of drawers.

Indicative of Baltimore cabinetmaking, the desk facade is a combination of inlaid satinwood ovals and rectangles set into dark panels. Triangular pediments topped with wooden balls on plinths rest on the two pedestal cabinets. Turned legs of thin scale support these pedestals and are graced with an extremely fine-gauge spiralled double-line inlay.

Not pictured in Sheraton's sketch is the *verre églomisé* that adorns the glass panels. Each glass cabinet is reverse

painted, or painted from the back so that the design appears on the front. This decoration provides another clue to the piece's Baltimore origins. The motifs, gilt foliage and a female allegorical figure encircled with a repetitive triangular border, embody the heart of Neoclassical decoration.

The Baltimore attribution becomes even likelier with the discovery of a pencilled inscription on a drawer bottom that reads: "M. Oliver Married the 5 October 1811, Baltimore." This piece remains as one of the most exceptional forms in Federal America. The Metropolitan Museum of Art in New York now owns this secretary.

A cherry with mahogany bookcase now at Winterthur from the Hartford, Connecticut, area seems at first glance to be a Chippendale form recycled with new ornament. The broken scroll pediment, slant top, bracket feet and serpentine lower case are essentially Chippendale. However, the delicate fretwork of the pediment, as well as the highly repetitive chevron stringing around the doors and drawers, point to an early nineteenth-century origin.

In addition to the chevron bands, the doors of the bookcase are inset with small fan inlays in the corners. Inverted icicle-shaped inlays on the sides and the carved urn of the pediment recall motifs seen on chairs made for the Hartford State House.

Additional ornament in the shape of vines and floral inlay, some of it sprouting from an urn on the fall-board, adds another dimension of Neoclassical emphasis to the case. Like japanning that was more advanced than the forms with which it was often paired, innovative inlay work such as this is an example of ornament more advanced than underlying form.

By far the most arresting ornament is found at eye level. Two eagles with shields are centered in the panels of the doors. With their outspread wings, these highly stylized birds are sometimes thought to be the definitive motif of American Federal furniture. The eagle motif appeared everywhere from inlay patterns to finials and in all categories throughout the decorative arts. In 1782 the Continental Congress selected the bald eagle as the national emblem. Nevertheless, any attribution based on this motif alone would be overzealous. English work of the period also incorporated the eagle.

The eagle motif was simply a part of the larger opus of Neoclassical ornament—it actually dates back to antiquity. Looking glasses adorned with carved and/or gilded eagles are frequently misattributed as being American. Collectors should exercise caution in accepting attribution based solely on this motif.

Another form new to the period was the tambour desk, a specialty of Massachusetts cabinetmakers. In form, the tambour desk is a close relative of the French *bonheur-du-jour,* a desk with a flat cabinet and a fall front that stands on legs. The tambour is a compact secretary with sliding doors of heavy cloth on which thin vertical strips of wood have been glued. Both versions offer the features of a desk in a space-saving compartment.

The Seymour name is closely linked with the handful of tambour desks extant, although recent scholarship has helped differentiate true Seymour attributes from imitators. Typical of Seymour work is fine inlay rendered so effectively that the eye sees movement through the integration of light and dark patterns. These contrasts are so elusive that the full effect of their beauty is best seen in person rather than through a photograph.

OPPOSITE PAGE: *The exceptionally delicate lacelike fretwork of the pediment and the repetitive chevron stringing around the doors and drawers of this cherry and mahogany secretary-bookcase from Connecticut allude to an early nineteenth-century design.* BELOW: *Recognized as the* "Sister's Cylinder Bookcase" *after Plate 38 in Sheraton's* The Cabinet Dictionary, *this H-shaped secretary-bookcase is the most ambitious piece of furniture after an English design. It embodies Federal taste in early nineteenth-century Baltimore.*

These desks are elegant yet amazingly simple inside and out. Behind the tambour doors, valanced pigeonholes preside over a series of drawers. The interior of the pigeonholes was often painted a robin's egg blue, another idiosyncracy associated with the Seymours.

Different in form but similar in usage is a group of small Baltimore desks referred to as ladies' cabinets and writing tables. There are three surviving examples based on Plate 50 of Sheraton's 1793 *Drawing Book.*

Stripped of ornament, any one of these would qualify as a modest desk and cabinet of banal geometric forms. With the addition of satinwood banding and five painted and gilded allegorical figures, it is a tour de force. Such decorative pieces stand on straight, tapered legs.

The single most important innovation in Federal furniture was the sideboard. As rooms became more specialized in the early nineteenth century, no dining room was complete without one. In the sideboard's compartments were housed linens, bottles, and serving pieces that when in use were laid out with precise adherence to rule books. Both Hepplewhite and Sheraton lauded the sideboard's function.

New York produced the largest sideboards, with standard measurements having a length of six feet (180 cm),

a width of two feet six inches (75 cm), and a depth of twenty-one inches (52 cm). Philadelphia's models were often a foot (30 cm) shorter and six inches (15 cm) less deep. Maryland and the South showed a preference for the huntboard over the sideboard.

The huntboard is a sideboard table without drawers, or with a single row of drawers under the top. These narrow tables were often accompanied by a separate cellarette to house the bottles that would have been stored in the deep drawers of the sideboard.

With the advent of technology came changes in cabinet-making techniques. For the first time it became possible to use glued layers of wood in a manner that allowed the greatest degree of expression in form and in ornament.

In the Federal period, the sideboard was a low, horizontally configured cabinet that stood against a wall or was placed in an alcove. Standing on straight, tapered legs or on turned and reeded legs, the cabinet ranged from the flat-surfaced to models with serpentine, D-shaped, and concave surfaces.

Regional tendencies also surfaced in sideboard form and ornament. Boston examples reflected the conservative taste of the homes in which they were placed. A mahogany-

This mahogany sideboard with boxwood, ebony, and satinwood inlay bears witness to the exalted level to which Baltimore cabinetmaking climbed to after the Revolution. The pictorial inlay in the center arch and the églomisé panels define Baltimore casework of the finest order.

veneered sideboard, circa 1800, at the Museum of Fine Arts in Boston, defines Boston taste.

The body is a rectangular box containing three drawers across the width of the case. The drawers are mounted with brass ring pulls. Beneath the drawers are three cabinet compartments with tambour doors.

The quality of the flame inlay strongly suggests that the Seymour firm had a hand in its design. Curly maple, cherry, rosewood, and stainwood were employed with just enough frequency as to provide the subtle accents that Bostonians relished.

The case is enhanced with carving in shallow relief just below the top at each of the corners and on the legs. It is likely that the carving was done by a specialist, since in the best shops the procedure acknowledged the strong points of each craftsman in the multistep nineteenth-century process.

Simple pendants at the bottom of the case seem almost superfluous yet they resemble the pendants seen on Seymour-ascribed sideboards. Minute inlaid ivory urns surround the keyhole escutcheons. Such details help to separate the best examples from those of pedestrian quality.

A New York cabinetmaking shop relied instead on representational inlay and angled corners to present its decorative synopsis, as did some shops in Philadelphia,

Baltimore, and the South. This contrasts with the broad and flat surface of the Boston example.

Underlying components were universal to all sideboards. A rectangular box horizontally laid out was finished with a series of drawers and cabinets. Typical of New York sideboards was heavy use of light-colored quarter fan inlay, paterae, fans, swags, and pendant husks against boldly figured mahogany.

Most sideboards stand on six legs—four at each corner and two inner or front legs to provide support for the piece's width, especially where there is a change in the direction of the cabinet. Masterful examples from New York have been found with eight legs, where the maker has placed a total of four in front.

These extra legs appear in conjunction with cantered corners. An unusual New York area feature is the presence of diagonally set inner legs that follow the cantered corners of the case.

A mahogany sideboard with boxwood, ebony, and satinwood inlay made in Baltimore, circa 1795–1800, and now at New York's Metropolitan Museum of Art, stands as a further testament to the exalted level to which Baltimore cabinetmaking climbed after the Revolution. Along with a handful of other Baltimore case pieces, it is among the most elaborate of all Federal furniture.

Seating ∽

Courtesy The Metropolitan Museum of Art, NYC, gift of Mrs. J. Insley Blair, 1947

This oval-back side chair with Prince of Wales plumes was the best that money could buy. Elias Hasket Derby ordered a large set of these chairs for his Salem home. The spade feet and inclined rear legs are found on the best Salem chairs.

As previously noted, chair forms are often the purest expression of an aesthetic. Federal chairs do not belie this rule; they are the apotheosis of classical ornament applied to contemporary form.

Federal chairs were light in form or substructure. Veneers, inlay, and low-relief carving of small and delicate scale made judicious use of the entire range of Federal design.

In Federal America, side chairs were designed with one of three basic back shapes: shield-back, square-back, and oval-back. These shapes were a design standard through the first decade of the nineteenth century.

The shield-back chair was the most popular form in Boston, Salem, and throughout New England. In period terminology, the shield-back was referred to as a "vase back" if the bottom of the shield was pointed, and an "urn back" when the bottom of the shield was rounded.

Seats are square and are wider in front than in back. Plain or gently bowed rails secured these seats. Most seats were over-upholstered. Brass tacks often in a swag pattern secured the covering. Green was the most popular upholstery color. Haircloth was the commonest covering, followed by thinly tanned leather dyed red, blue, green, or black.

Wools and silks were also popular but survive less frequently today due to insect damage. Printed cotton was sometimes employed to make slipcovers for summer usage.

Tapered legs, many with stretchers, are found on some New England chairs. Legs were unadorned or highlighted with several strings of light-colored wood. Reeded legs on Boston chairs are rare. Spade feet are found on the finest Salem chairs, usually in conjunction with carving and appliqués of exotic woods; in these chairs stretchers are conspicuously absent, as are inlays.

Salem chairs also have rear legs that gently incline inward so that the distance between the rear legs is noticeably smaller than the distance between the front legs. The highest style Salem chairs were to be found in the Derby home.

Several chairs of this special group are in the Museum of Fine Arts in Boston. One chair, circa 1795, based on Plate 2 of Hepplewhite's *Guide* is a shield-back chair with a central urn motif flanked by two thin vertical slats containing small flower ovals or paterae that emanate from a lunette at the base of the shield. Beyond the gracefulness of its form (by a hand yet to be named), the most distinguishing feature is the abundant and beautiful carving that has been attributed to Samuel McIntire.

Typical McIntire finesse features a carved grapevine motif down the front legs, a motif that appears on numerous other objects from the Derby household. The basket of fruit in the demilune inset at the bottom of the chair back is another McIntire trademark of furniture design. Befitting its stature, the chair was finished with spade feet covered with ebony.

An oval-back painted chair with six Prince of Wales feathers painted in polychrome is part of a set originally ordered by Elias Hasket Derby. The soft maple and white pine frame is covered with an allover dark brown-black paint.

110 AMERICAN ANTIQUE FURNITURE

LEFT: *Made en suite with matching side chairs and a double chair-back settee, this mahogany five-chair-back settee is attributed to the Seymour shop of Boston. The combination of squares, rectangles, ellipses, and diamonds demonstrates the thinness to which Federal pieces ascribed.* BELOW: *Duncan Phyfe's one-hundred-person shop turned out New York scroll-back armchairs, with decorative enhancements that included thin zig-zag bands intersected with rosettes, reeded legs, and the bowknot motif on the crest.*

Six ostrich feathers make up the Prince of Wales plumes. The polychrome paint that depicts flowers and ribbon satisfied the penchant for delicate painted furniture that surfaced briefly in the Boston-Salem area from 1790 to 1805.

This chair, along with others from the set, is somewhat problematical in terms of origin. Some scholars believe the group of chairs was made in Massachusetts; others once thought the chairs were made in Philadelphia because they were believed to be linked to a bill of sale by Joseph Anthony & Company of Philadelphia.

For all its delicacy, the chair has an ample over-upholstered seat that symbolically mirrors the ample fortune of the family for whom the set was commissioned. Regardless of problems of attribution, this chair joins one at the Metropolitan Museum of Art and one at Winterthur Museum that are admired as much for their rarity as for their beauty.

Square-back chairs were found less frequently in Massachusetts. The form found better expression in Portsmouth, New Hampshire, and in New York. Portsmouth chairs have square, reeded backs with rosettes at the corners of the crest, tapered and molded front legs, outcurved rear legs, and stretchers.

Another form, the scroll-back chair, made around 1805, prefigured the reappearance of the graceful *klismos,* an ancient Greek chair of classical form. The klismos became the most popular form in the Empire period. In his

FEDERAL STYLE 111

New York workshop, Duncan Phyfe modelled his scroll-back chair after the klismos.

The Boston version has a scrolled back and splayed legs. The chair is topped with a small horizontal roller with a tablet on top. These extremely sophisticated chairs —the only Massachusetts chairs with thin, half over-upholstered seats—have been attributed to the shop of John and Thomas Seymour due to the high quality of the carving and contrasting light birch veneers that are worked into the mahogany.

A pair of these chairs was made en suite with a five-chair-back settee, or a settee that visually resembles five chair backs in one piece. The Seymour set is a symphony of contrasts between light and dark woods, plain and carved surfaces, and geometric forms on backs made up of squares, half and quarter ellipses, rectangles, and diamonds.

Rhode Island buyers favored a chair with a pedestal or modified square back whose silhouette easily recalls a Chippendale chair, as does the central splat, which is so close to a pierced splat. The central splat rests on a pedestal or shoe, another trait associated with the older style.

This chair does not seem to have a precedent in either Hepplewhite's or Sheraton's sketches. Rather, it seems to follow an example illustrated in *The London Chair-Makers' and Carvers' Book of Prices for Workmanship* of 1802.

The legs are tapered and are usually connected by H-shaped stretchers. They are finished with large over-upholstered seats. The favorite motif of the center splat is the kylix, a flattened, horizontally displayed urn from which drapery has been extruded. On these chairs, large pendant bellflowers flow down from the bottom of the urn, and in their distorted scale, expose the hand of the provincial maker who produced it.

Connecticut chairmakers produced variants of this form with Chippendale style silhouettes, stiles, rails, and Marlborough legs. They integrated them with the more up-to-date flat Adamesque urn and swag-studded tack patterns.

As a point of scholarship, furniture that mixes elements from several styles is sometimes termed "transitional" and can present problems in dating. Some furniture is indeed transitional; such pieces mix components because the tenets of the new style are not yet understood by the maker. Other pieces mix elements from differing periods for cost considerations, simple turned pad feet on a Chippendale chair, for example. To avoid the dating confusion that the term transitional can create, it is sometimes more productive to think in terms of the most current attributes. The object can then be dated by its most recent feature.

For example, on a chair that has simple pad feet (first seen on Queen Anne furniture from 1725 to 1755) and a pierced splat and scrolled ears (Chippendale features) one can determine that the chair must be a product of the Chippendale period, or the period with the chair's most current features. The chair can then be dated from 1755 to 1790, and the period may even be narrowed down based on other attributes or documentation.

New York chairmakers constructed three varieties of shield-back chair forms. The first group had backs with banisters of three splats centering a fan. The second type mixed Prince of Wales feathers with drapery. Lastly, there were backs with four ribs.

A different form, the square-back, was most often paired with center banisters with an elongated urn, feathers, and drapery, all of which was flanked by colonnettes. On some models, the colonnettes meshed with gothic arches at the top. Armchairs of this type with outward flaring arm supports are infrequently finished with carved rosettes at the junction with the arm. New Yorkers showed a particular affinity for this type.

Carving and reeding were used as decorative devices to a great degree in New York. A sunburst tablet at the top of the New York square-back chair is integral to the design. This contrasts with Philadelphia versions, in which the tablet simply rests on the top of the crest.

The New York scroll-back chair, like its Seymour-attributed counterpart in Boston, became a popular form about 1800. It, too, was based on the klismos, the ancient Greek chair with a splayed back and saber legs whose simplicity and beauty of outline have never been surpassed.

One of the earliest appearances of this form in New York is documented by a bill of sale dated November 21, 1807, from Duncan Phyfe to a wealthy New Yorker, William Bayard, for his house on State Street. Many pieces from the original group are housed in Winterthur's Phyfe Room. The klismos chair was so popular that Phyfe's shop had more than one hundred workers turning out these chairs.

Enhancements to the form that add an extra degree of appeal include zig-zag bands with rosettes, reeding on the front legs, and the bowknot motif on the crest. Seats followed a bell or slightly rounded shape and were over-upholstered. Eventually, the form would expand into the lyre and harp-back motif and take easily to the archaeological correctness of the approaching Empire style.

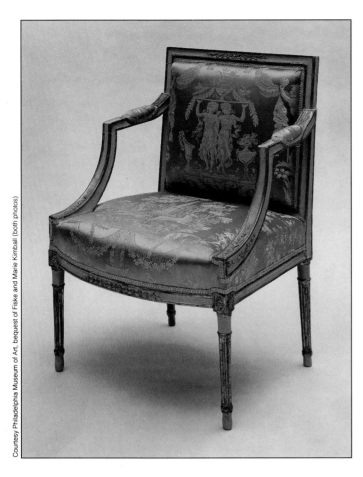

A square-back chair listed in a Philadelphia price book as "with straight top and stay rail, three upright splats, straight seat, made for stuffing over the rails" describes a chair with turned legs ending in bulb or round spade feet. This was a form with great appeal in Philadelphia.

In 1807, Ephraim Haines charged the French-born financier Stephen Girard, one of Philadelphia's wealthiest inhabitants, $500 for a set of similarly conceived black ebony furniture. The furniture is today preserved at Girard College in Philadelphia.

The squared back with three turned, reeded, and carved banisters or columns owes a debt to the spirit of classicism. Armchairs were more difficult to execute successfully, so they captured a premium price. Haines along with his peer, Henry Connelly, are known for the high rising arms called "French elbows" after those found on French furniture of the Louis XVI style.

A select group of gilded armchairs formed another variant of Philadelphia chairs. Although Sheraton once described chairs with painted and glided finishes, the appearance of such highly decorative specimens in Philadelphia probably coincides with the importation of French prototypes.

These monumental armchairs were painted white and gold. They had upholstered backs and partially upholstered arm supports as well as applied composition ornament. Hepplewhite referred to upholstered back chairs as cabriole chairs, while Sheraton referred to them as drawing room chairs.

One of the closest expressions of French Louis XVI style, this armchair and painted sofa from Philadelphia would have appealed to francophiles including Jefferson, Monroe, and Adams.

Carving on these ambitious chairs was of the highest quality. It is a certainty that seating pieces such as these would have been reserved exclusively for the best parlor.

Baltimore's rocketing fortunes have been well chronicled in the discussion of its high-style case work discussed above. Popular chair forms there included the shield-back, the heart-back, and the oval-back, which was extremely rare outside of Baltimore.

Adam is touted as having introduced oval-backs to England, where they were popular from the 1760s to the 1780s. The exclusivity of this form to Baltimore only strengthens the observation that Baltimore furniture was the most "English" of all Federal furniture.

Some Baltimore modified shield-backs incorporate a balloon shape, or one that resembles a head of a tennis racket. These were close versions of examples in Sheraton's *Drawing Book*.

When paired with ingredients such as a partially over-upholstered seat, H-shaped stretchers stringing across the lower edge of the seat rail, and light-wood bands or cuffs on tapered legs, they point to a Baltimore origin, as does carrot-shaped inlay on leg fronts.

John and Hugh Finlay advertised in 1805 that they could produce "cane seat chairs, sofas, recess and window seats of every description and all colors, gilt, ornamented and varnished in a stile not equalled on the continent—with real Views, Fancy Landscapes, Flowers, Trophies of Music, War, Husbandry, Love, &c. &c." They were later commissioned during the Madison Administration to execute a suite of furniture for the President's house.

A select group of polychrome painted "fancy" chairs, tables, and settees fit this description. They also satisfied the Baltimore thirst for pictorial ornament.

What some Baltimore cabinetmakers achieved with pictorial inlay of contrasting wood and *verre églomisé*, the Finlays achieved with polychrome paint. These chairs as a genre later inspired less expensive versions, including the famous mass-produced, painted and stencilled Hitchcock chair that retailed for $1.50 and brought a certain degree of style to middle-class homes.

As one can see from an example at the Metropolitan Museum of Art in New York, the painting technique that the Finlays perfected was applied to Sheraton forms. Besides the painted surface, another Finlay trait is icicle-shaped splats. One piece of the group commissioned, a chair, was built from mahogany and maple. The body was painted black, with gilt and multicolored decoration.

In Charleston, the shield-back was fashionable. It was sometimes enhanced with drapery carving that has also been found on New York and Massachusetts chairs. This seems logical since Charleston increased its importation of furniture from these two northern cities at this time.

Scholarship continues to bring to light more southern cabinetmakers. The search has been somewhat obscured due to the use of slave labor that was common in the South's early furniture industry.

Other seating forms include the easy chair and the lolling chair. Seating forms that accommodated more than one person include the sofa and the settee, of which both forms reached high points of design in the early nineteenth century.

The easy chairs continually reflected regional taste, but in general, they were thinner overall in appearance compared to models of the Queen Anne and Chippendale periods. Upholstery mass was spare, often held in check by the tightly sewn "French edge" that gave Federal upholstered pieces a precise line or edge.

In New England, straight rolled arms and straight legs prevailed. New York favored soft C-scroll arms and cylindrical legs; Philadelphia models frequently had reeded legs and bulb feet, deep wings and circular, rounded backs. Baltimore versions had downward sloping arms.

The lolling chair, an upholstered armchair, was also known as a "Martha Washington chair." The term lolling was early nineteenth-century description for any indulgent, leisurely activity. The reason for the association with Martha Washington has been lost over the years and remains merely suggestive of the distinctly American style of the chair.

These chairs, with their tall backs and slim, tapered arms and legs, were the domain of New England chairmakers. Massachusetts produced the greatest number of them.

The sofa, having grown more popular from the Chippendale period, nevertheless continued to be a luxury reserved for the wealthiest of households. While sofas varied according to personal taste and to the size of the room in which they were situated, many of this time followed dimensions of six to seven feet (180 to 210 cm) in length, thirty inches (75 cm) in depth, and a back height of about three feet (90 cm).

Compared to their Chippendale antecedents, Federal sofas had a tendency toward delicate proportions. Some had serpentine backs accessorized with wood; others had bowed or "sweeped" backs. Baltimore examples of this form were called cabriole sofas.

Another coveted form was a square sofa with turned arm supports. Exposed arms were new to the period. Federal sofas were outlined with mahogany embellished with veneer, reeding, or carving. Front legs were square, turned, or tapered.

OPPOSITE PAGE: *A polychrome painted "fancy" chair and table by John and Hugh Finlay were the nineteenth-century equivalents of japanned furniture and satisfied the Baltimore passion for pictorial ornament. The icicle-shaped splats on the chair are another Finlay trait.*
RIGHT: *Federal sofas, while gaining in popularity, were still a luxury largely reserved for the wealthy. Compared to earlier Chippendale and Queen Anne designs, Federal sofas had a tendency toward delicate scale.*

Courtesy The Henry Francis du Pont Winterthur Museum, DE

Tables ❧

Courtesy The Henry Francis du Pont Winterthur Museum, DE

To an already abundant supply of table types, two new forms were added. One was the dining table, the appearance of which coincided with that of a room designated exclusively for dining.

Federal dining tables, which were usually of the drop-leaf variety, do not survive with as great a frequency as do other table types. Part of the reason for their early demise is due to the stress that was exerted on the frame when the long expanse of leaves was extended.

Sometimes two or more drop-leaf tables were joined in groups to form seating space for up to ten people. Other tables were three-part configurations with two half-round ends or aprons capable of separate service. These large halves were supported by four square and tapered legs. Later models had D-shaped ends and six turned and tapered legs.

Another form introduced during the Federal period was a small table, usually with a drawer and a large storage area for fabric and sewing implements. It is called a sewing table, or more accurately, a work table. Sheraton called them pouch tables, but this description was not widely used in America.

New England work tables made more than frequent use of canted corners and stood on square, tapered, or round legs, some with elongated bulbous feet and ring turnings at the tops of legs. Salem examples employed many of these features on delicate frames.

Stringing helped to accentuate contrasting veneers of birch or satinwood against mahogany. Rarely, Boston examples were decorated with fine floral motifs rendered in paint that reflected the short-lived fad, which in Boston never reached the fervor that it did in Baltimore.

Philadelphia work tables were made in several forms, including the oval and astragal-end shape. Astragal-end tables have a protruding front and back that interrupt a basic oval shape.

Mahogany and satinwood were the preferred primary woods; on satinwood models, darker rosewood or ebony banding and stringing around panels and drawers is commonly found. Unique to Philadelphia was the kidney-shaped work table, the most prized examples of which reside at Winterthur Museum and in the Garvan Collection at Yale University.

The same beauty of form, material, and workmanship that once distinguished the Philadelphia Chippendale highboy resurfaced in the kidney-shaped work table.

Baltimore artisans produced oval and square work tables usually in mahogany. Baltimore, like Philadelphia, emphasized panels and drawers with light woods.

New York shops supplied canted corner work tables, and the astragal-end table, which was in great demand. Dark, richly figured mahogany presented a solid surface. The scale was slightly larger and the case rested on saber legs. Light wood stringing was used with less intensity.

Lannuier and Phyfe each interpreted the work table differently but they both shared a penchant for excellence of materials and workmanship. Phyfe seemed to prefer a large square work table with canted corners and a large singular case on saber legs.

Lannuier relied on his French heritage to produce a work table that showed the thin, rectangular emphasis of late eighteenth-century French cabinet work. One can compare the attributes of each of these tables at the Winterthur Museum.

Eventually, Lannuier and Phyfe both followed the trend toward archaeological accuracy in the Empire period. While Phyfe's early Neoclassical work is readily distinguishable from Lannuier's, their later pieces are less so.

A card table in the early stages of American Neoclassicism was made in one of four shapes: square, round, tripod, and pedestal. As a holdover from their Chippendale origins, many circular New York card tables had five legs; rarer models had six. Some Federal card tables appear to have been made in pairs, following the Neoclassical mandate for symmetry in room arrangement.

In the tradition established by case pieces, New England card tables had satinwood and birch veneers, often with an oval panel centered on front. This gave the illusion of three sections across the front and provided excellent contrasts of light and dark.

Early Boston and Salem card tables came with serpentine, elliptic, or bowed fronts. About 1800, serpentine fronts were modelled with ovolo corners that conformed to the shape of the turned front legs. Federal card tables were finished with a significant amount of ornament. Many examples originally wore labels from the shops where they were assembled. A circular card table by John Townsend of Newport demonstrates this point. The table, at the Winterthur Museum, has the label John Townsend of Newport and is inscribed 1796. The mahogany body is accentuated with light and dark stringing of the most subdued kind.

OPPOSITE PAGE: The kidney-shaped work table was a highly coveted prize in Philadelphia. Rich ebony inlay accentuates the biomorphic shape of the satinwood body on perhaps the most exquisite one of its kind. **ABOVE:** *This work table attributed to John and Thomas Seymour has legs of very delicate thinness.*
RIGHT: *The fine-painted floral motif attributed to John Penniman was the expression of a short-lived fad in Boston at the beginning of the nineteenth century.*

Courtesy Israel Sack, Inc., NYC

This extremely graceful mahogany lyre-base card table with canted corners and well-poised outsplayed legs is the epitome of the Neoclassical ideal. Based on the drapery panel that is related to one on a Sheraton card table, this New York model is attributed to Michael Allison.

Light-colored book inlays on the apron and on both tapered legs resemble the fronts of horizontally stacked books. Flared bellflower husks with black-veined lines and paterae are other Newport quirks.

Baltimore tables showed the greatest degree of ornamental choices. This was due in part to the regional inlay artistry that flourished there. The aesthetic package was wrapped in contrasting veneers that many times were in the form of light-colored wide stretches of ovals. Shading sometimes replaced contrasts of light against dark for different visual impact.

Other earmarks of Baltimore tables include satinwood teardrop panels, three-part husks on legs with elongated center petals, flower and vase inlays, carrot-shaped inlays on legs, stylized tassels, and urns.

Rich veneers are what catch the eye first on New York card tables. Dark mahogany made up the largest percentage of these veneers and was used repetitively from the top to the body and legs.

The New York rendering of the bellflower inlay was strung with ovals. *Églomisé* panels, although strongly linked with Baltimore, have been found on tables with New York histories. New York consumers also showed a taste for looking glasses with *églomisé* panels.

A square table bearing the label of Charles-Honoré Lannuier reflects not only excellence of workmanship, but more importantly, the influence of French design on American Federal furniture. New York was second only to Philadelphia in its taste for things French.

Trained in France, Lannuier continued to follow the French practice of labelling or stamping his work. One table that summarizes Lannuier's early style in America was derived initially from French Neoclassicism, especially the Directoire style, which was essentially a simplified version of the Louis XVI style. The table was less ornate and was adorned with motifs that symbolized the French Revolution, including the wreath.

Another distinctive New York card table is the pedestal table with a five-lobed or double elliptic top and carved tripod base. Legs end in paw feet that are finished in brass or are carved from solid wood. The form, dated about 1810, was once exclusively attributed to the hand of Duncan Phyfe. Later study has shown that the form was made and sold by a group of New York cabinetmakers. *The New York Revised Prices for Manufacturing Cabinet and Chair Work* of 1810 bears out this group attribution.

The decorative effect of this table is dependent on the flame of the mahogany and on the stylized leaf carving on the base. The underlying form harkens back to many pillar-and-claw tables.

Philadelphia card tables fell into two major categories. A circular card table dated about 1790, made by Jonathan Gostelowe, has larger scale, knee brackets, and fluted Marlborough legs ending in blocky feet that are carryovers from the Chippendale style.

By 1810, the form had changed radically. The new shape is related to the five-lobed pedestal base table from New York, with some obvious differences.

The Philadelphia top is displaced over a wider area; four colonnettes substitute for a single pedestal. The Philadelphia base has four molded legs with leaf carving instead of three; the Philadelphia base is more rounded and convex.

Although it has not been documented with certainty, Henry Connelly and Ephraim Haines have been suggested as possible makers of this table. When opened, the top has a sunburst pattern of eighteen figured mahogany rays similar to those found on a pair of tables made for Stephen Girard. It resides at Winterthur. When the baton was passed to Empire stylists, the scale of these tables grew.

Bedsteads

igh-post bedsteads were still draped with fabric but by the beginning of the nineteenth century, it was no longer common to totally enrobe the bed with draperies. Hangings were based on illustrations from Hepplewhite's *Guide;* canopies with cascading tails and back panels were restrained enough in volume as to let the turned and reeded footposts of the bed show.

In accord with the strict dictates of Neoclassical design, window treatments were selected with a keen eye toward harmonizing with the shape, color, and texture of the bed hangings. In a change from traditions in New England and in New York, Philadelphia rear footposts and headboards were ornamented to match the front.

Bedsteads with mahogany rails and moveable headboards are usually attributed to a Charleston origin. Field beds continued to be made into the Federal period and their frames took a serpentine outline that replaced the straight or arched frames that came before them.

A rare example of a four-post bedstead with its original finish, rails, headboard, and tester frame, this Salem bedstead, circa 1800 to 1810, would have been dressed in fabric restrained enough in volume to let the reeded footposts show.

Empire Style

(1815–1840)

Go forth, and rival Greece's art sublime; Return, and bid the statesmen of thy land Live in thy marble through all after-time!

John Quincy Adams to the American sculptor Hiram Powers

By conquest, treaty, or purchase, the United States was continuing its territorial expansion. The collective attitude of the people was one of incessant optimism, instilling a patriotic belief that the nation was finally in command of its fate.

In the realm of furniture design approximating the years 1815 to 1840, other conquests were occurring: Plasticity conquered flatness, boldness overtook fineness, and restraint capitulated to heavy ornament. The resultant Empire style that developed was the second phase of the Neoclassical period of furniture-making in America.

In the beginning it assumed an archaeological correctness that separated Empire work from earlier Federal furniture. From about 1825 to 1840, archaeological accuracy dissolved, resulting in large-scale pieces, the heftiest forms of which were dubbed "fat classical."

During the Empire era, furniture forms swelled from the delicate Hepplewhite- and Sheraton-inspired furniture of the first decade of the nineteenth century. Solid, large-scale furniture predominated, if only to accommodate the archaeological motifs that were used as decoration.

rotate

Courtesy Metropolitan Museum of Art, NYC, gift of Joe Kindig, Jr., 1968/photo by Richard Cheek

Style Overview

Courtesy Woldman & Woldman, Alexandria, VA

The urge toward archaeological precision was not limited to decoration; underlying forms required archaeological correctness as well. The Greek *klismos,* a chair with outcurved saber legs and a concave back that curved to accommodate the spine, formed the basis for much Empire style chair design.

The *curule,* or X-shaped base, was another classical element that found its way into contemporary furniture. There was an emphasis on monumentality; objects looked as if they had just been carved from stone.

A number of different influences contributed to the evolution of the American Empire style. The term Empire refers to the period in French history when Napoleon assumed control—1804 to 1815. That the title carried over to furniture design only serves to underscore Napoleon's vast influence, even in the decorative arts. The appreciation of serious archaeological classicism via the study of ancient Greece and Rome couldn't have been better timed for the neo-conqueror Napoleon. Through the work of his designers, Charles Percier and Pierre Fontaine, the Empire style metastasized.

Percier and Fontaine often travelled with Napoleon's troops so that they could make scale drawings of the furniture that inspired the designs of the Empire. They included elements from many great cultures—Roman, Greek, and Egyptian—to satisfy the vanity of Napoleon.

In scale and in ornament, this treasure chest of Neoclassicism achieved an expression far more grandiose than anything inspired by Hepplewhite and Sheraton. Lofty motifs appeared, with military symbols such as the sword and shield that recalled the glory of Imperial Rome.

Also depicted were winged caryatid figures, lion's paw feet, and the monopodium leg. The monopodium leg combined the attributes of an animal head with an animal paw foot in a single arrangement.

Percier and Fontaine published their illustrations in *Recueil des Décorations Intérieures* in 1801 and again in 1812. Jacques-Louis David, court painter to Napoleon, painted innumerable portraits and historical scenes complete with furniture in *le style antique.* His portrait of Juliette Récamier on a Grecian couch is regarded as an icon of Neoclassicism.

As the patterns of Hepplewhite and Sheraton drew inspiration from the brothers Adam in the Federal period, so Percier and Fontaine had the example of Pierre de la Mésangère, who popularized the rudiments of Empire style into manageable and affordable designs for a wide-ranging public. His *Collection des Meubles et Objets de Goût* was published continuously in France until 1835.

Percier and Fontaine's influence spread to England, where it was promoted by their friend, Thomas Hope. In 1807, Hope, an antiquarian, published *Household Furniture and Interior Decoration.* Its illustrations laid out furniture with the same archaeological literacy that typified the French Empire style. He was later joined by a host of others who helped disseminate archaeological classicism to English dilettantes.

In England, the manifestation of archaeological classicism is referred to as the Regency style, dating roughly from 1800 to 1838, approximately the period when George, Prince of Wales, acted as Regent for his ailing father, George III, before ascending the throne.

As with the generations of furniture styles that precede it, the American Empire style is a selective blending of form and ornament from more than one source. Like the melting pot image that represents the ethnic makeup of the country, the end result was a highly distinctive, additive style that today is easily recognizable as American.

OPPOSITE PAGE: *Attributed to Joseph Meeks & Sons, this New York pier table of 1825 is a dazzling blend of carving, gilding, and stencilling on a singular Empire form.* **ABOVE:** *The Greek* klismos *was the prototype for most Empire chair designs. This Finlay painted maple example is a skillful compromise between the delicate proportions of ancient Greek models and a more masculine Roman version.*

From the English Regency style, American craftsmen selected pillars, brass paw feet and casters, reeding, waterleaf carving, and dolphins. Gilt mounts, swags, and Egyptian details, on the other hand, were borrowed from French Empire objects.

Much of this blending of detail can be traced to the diverse design vocabularies of the immigrant craftsmen who brought particular styles with them. Some of these aesthetic liberties can also be explained by the unique philosophical predisposition and taste in America.

Having emerged only recently from their colonial status, Americans could never totally adopt the imperial style of the French Empire. Nor could they entirely accept the English Regency style that grew out of the Adamesque, a style that in England outshined its American successors in ornament and in cost.

American furniture consequently pays homage to this multiplicity of sources in a peculiarly American way. The painted and gilded furniture of the period illustrates this point succinctly. Craftsmen ingeniously substituted gold-leaf decoration and stencilling for the expensive brass mounts of French Empire examples. Paint could occasionally substitute for the more exotic marble or ebony.

A secretary in New York's Metropolitan Museum of Art built by the New York firm of Joseph Meeks & Sons dates to 1825, and stands more than eight feet (240 cm) tall. The ebonized mahogany body, with its columns and cornice, resembles a temple facade. The hefty case stands on huge animal paw feet that connect to the lower case with gilded cornucopia brackets.

Additional gilding on the columns helps to balance the composition and to orient the eyes upward. Other high-style points include brass mullions that decorate the glass doors, pleated silk curtains, and repetitive stencilling that mimics costly French *ormolu* (decorative bronze).

Large-scale floral stencilling elsewhere on the body is more free-form than the tight, repetitive patterns that highlight the drawers and doors. This stencilling appears to be almost an afterthought, and is therefore less successful than the small stencilling, and portrays a more provincial decorative attitude. The extremely large scale of the piece can carry it, so its overall negative effect is minimal on an otherwise impressive piece.

In addition to the motifs mentioned above, clues that portend a shift from the Federal style, or early stage of Neoclassicism, to the Empire style include the change in scale. Forms became heavier and bolder; a rich medley of carving resumed a sculptural, three-dimensional quality.

Inlay, the decorative process so strongly associated with Federal taste, disappeared from the reemerging curves of Empire forms. Neatly stencilled gilt borders simulating ormolu replaced the wooden bands of inlay. Brasses grew in proportion to the forms they adorned. The lion's head with a circular pull was especially prevalent.

Furniture makers still reached first for mahogany when building their pieces, but the harder- and higher-figured rosewood offered stiff competition, particularly after mid-century. The heavy contrasts of light and dark that were so pervasive in Federal furniture were passed over in favor of more richly figured solid surfaces. Geometric shapes were less important to the overall thematic intent of the Empire style, at least ornamentally.

Along with being heavier and bolder, case pieces once again revealed an architectural underpinning that was strong but didn't threaten the architectural slavishness of French Empire pieces. It was a variant of the architectural slant that had dictated Queen Anne and Chippendale cabinet work. Whereas those forms had tops that replicated pediments, Empire case pieces in totality often recalled the temple facade.

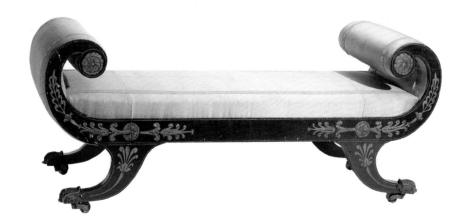

Baltimore turned out some of the most ornately decorated couches of the Empire period. Made from tulipwood, this couch has painted rosewood graining to simulate more expensive rosewood. The goldleaf was an innovative technique that gives the illusion of costly French ormolu.

Attributed to Joseph Meeks & Sons, this secretary-bookcase from New York reigns as the most bombastic
Empire design. Incorporated on its massive body are the disparate techniques of painting, carving,
stencilling, and gilding.

Case Pieces

Whether sideboards, secretary desks, or wardrobes, Empire case pieces were monumental in size and emphasized solidity of form. Typical of a sideboard was a heavy, geometric case of mahogany that stood close to the ground, often on short, thick, animal paw feet. The configurations of drawers and cabinets that marked the Federal sideboard looked totally different in the assertive Empire form.

Legs were notably different; from the slender versions on Federal cases they grew to columns of the five classical orders and were highlighted with diagonal or bulbous floral carving.

Fancier models might include options and embellishments such as a brass gallery around the top, brass inlay that alluded to the work of André-Charles Boulle, or matching knife boxes that followed the form and ornament of the sideboard.

The Philadelphia Museum of Art owns one of the most grandiloquent Philadelphia Empire sideboards. The mahogany veneer on this sideboard, usually fused to a less precious wood, was applied to a solid mahogany frame. The decorative statement comes from brass inlay set in ebony panels that draws its inspiration from boullework. A carved backboard and brass gallery add an interesting mix

of solid and void emphasis to an otherwise boxy shape.

This sideboard was made en suite with a matching pair of knife boxes and a cellarette for the Gratz family. While documentation is lacking for a firm attribution, it is posited that these pieces were made by Joseph Barry (1757–1839), the Philadelphia cabinetmaker who promoted the brass inlay technique.

A New York mahogany chest of drawers with an attached looking glass, a popular Empire form, has a massive geometric outline relieved only by the carved and scrolled brackets that support the mirror. Stencilled gilt borders around the drawers and mirror are an American bourgeois response to the more costly French ormolu.

The *secrétaire à abattant,* a Continental form with a fall-front desk, found its way to America directly from France without English modification. In America, the form was recognized as French, although on certain models, elements of Germanic influence are found, such as tabernacle tops and construction techniques. Popular from 1815 to about 1830, these sophisticated cabinet pieces reached their greatest level of popularity in the major style centers of New York, Philadelphia, and rarely, Boston.

OPPOSITE PAGE: *This Philadelphia sideboard of 1825 bespeaks quality from the mahogany veneers that are glued onto a solid mahogany frame to the brass and ebony inlay and carved backboard. Made with matching knife boxes and a cellarette for liquor, these pieces were a true tour de force.* **ABOVE:** *Based on a Continental form, the* secrétaire à abattant, *or desk with a fall-front writing surface, was popular mainly in New York, Philadelphia, and rarely, Boston.* **RIGHT:** *An example of how design elements from many cultures were affixed to furniture forms, this Egyptian-influenced elliptic chest uses highly figured mahogany and simple gilt brass pulls to express an archaeological quality. It is attributed to Joseph Barry & Son, Philadelphia, circa 1815.*

Seating ∾

The ancient Greek klismos chair, with its graceful lines and splayed legs, inspired this New York lyre-back chair. The form was particularly popular in the second stage of Neo-classicism, or the Empire.

The Greek klismos was the stylistic precursor of most Empire chairs. And while certain Empire forms were beginning to transcend regional boundaries, Empire chairs were the last pieces to incorporate generic traits.

In Boston, for example, chairmakers built a klismos chair with a carved swag and scrolled splat. The splat design, along with a twisted, reeded, and carved front rail, relies on the richness and depth of the mahogany for its beauty.

In Philadelphia, chairmakers discarded the illusion of an uninterrupted line from stiles to front legs that marks so many Boston and New York examples. The resultant form is a chair with larger proportions, resembling those illustrated by Hope. The sweeping back parallels similar designs executed by Benjamin Henry Latrobe for the White House.

As evidenced by their case pieces, Philadelphia cabinetmakers had a fondness for the revived art of boullework, which in its period was done with brass and ebony inlays. Approximately twelve chairs of this type dating to the second decade of the nineteenth century survive. The Museum of Fine Arts in Boston owns three chairs of mahogany painted to resemble rosewood. These Boston examples of the klismos have brass inlay and are delicately rendered.

New York klismos chairs ranged from models with simple scroll backs, little carving, and unadorned saber legs to those with reeded stiles, legs, or with carved and gilded animal paw feet.

Back decorations included the lyre, harp, cornucopia, or eagle. The best examples are usually attributed to Duncan Phyfe, but a number were the output of similarly skilled individuals, many of whom probably once worked in Phyfe's one-hundred-person shop.

The sling-seat armchair on a curule or X-shaped base looks surprisingly modern given its ancient heritage. The form was used in ancient Egypt as a sling seat over an X-shaped stretcher; Romans added more curve to the stretcher and converted it to seating for magistrates. Its simply joined clean lines and lack of fussiness give it an air of modernity.

In the seventeenth century, Spanish crafters added turned stretchers, curved arms, and leather upholstery to the form, thus creating the "campeachy" chair. Thomas Jefferson received a campeachy chair as a gift from a friend in New Orleans and later commissioned several of

ABOVE: *The campeachy chair looks surprisingly modern given its ancient heritage. Originally used in Egypt as a sling seat over an X-shaped stretcher, the form was modified to make a popular style appealing to nineteenth-century patrons, including Thomas Jefferson.* **RIGHT:** *Klismos chairs from Boston expressed that city's preference for plain expanses of rich mahogany veneer. Part of the appeal of these chairs is their inherently graceful outline.*

them for Monticello. He did much to popularize the form, which was favored throughout the period.

A side chair attributed to John and Hugh Finlay offers another look at a regional interpretation of the klismos form. This chair, at New York's Metropolitan Museum of Art, shares the heavier proportions of some Philadelphia models.

When combined with round tapering front legs, these features represent a Roman version of the famous Greek chair. In its original form, the klismos was often associated with women; the Romans modified the scale to accommodate the male figure. This reduced the original delicacy of the form.

The Finlay design is successful, however. It is a good compromise between the delicate proportions of the original Greek blueprint and a more masculine version as interpreted by the Romans.

Maple painted gold with black and green decoration relates the chair stylistically to a Baltimore chair once owned by the Alexander Brown family and now at the Museum of Fine Arts in Boston. The Museum of Fine Arts example uses the same shades, as well as the color red, to recreate the colors of Pompeii. Both the Finlay chair and the Brown family chair were influenced by Sheraton's 1802 edition of *The Cabinet-Maker and Upholsterer's Drawing Book.*

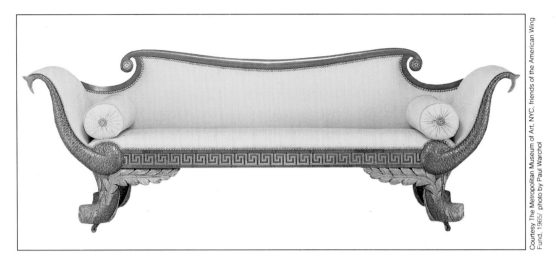

Made about 1820, this New York Grecian sofa, known as the "dolphin sofa" for its dolphin legs and scrolled arms, lacks no decorative detail. It is an exciting composition of sweeping curves and textural ornament.

In an aesthetic sense, sofas and couches demonstrated some of the best expressions of Empire equipage. Cabinetmakers had at their disposal innumerable pattern books to which they could look for guidance.

The terminology for these pieces can be confusing. Those seating forms with full backs were called sofas, while those with no backs or with partial backs were usually called couches. Couches filled the void left by daybeds.

Pattern books gave various names for this form; Sheraton once referred to it as the Grecian couch or Grecian squab. George Smith called them chaise lounges; Thomas Hope cited the Roman triclinium as a historical influence.

While there may be some confusion over names, the form's function was well understood. Unlike beds, couches and some sofas were made for short periods of repose—but not sleep. Like many card tables, they were sometimes made in pairs that flanked doorways or niches.

A Massachusetts sofa in the Museum of Fine Arts in Boston was copied almost verbatim from a popular 1821 London periodical, Ackermann's *Repository of Arts, Literature, Fashions, etc.* Shorter than many of its Federal antecedents, the sofa replicates the squared form and bulbous carving of Ackermann's example. Even the green silk upholstery is a close copy of the hand-colored Ackermann rendering. Its loose, overstuffed pillows contrast with the tight, linear look of Federal upholstery. On other examples, the universe of Empire upholstery expanded to include wool velvet.

A typical Philadelphia sofa had less ambitious scrolled ends with scroll legs and ormolu mounts. This contrasts

with New York examples that often employed wider scrolled arms and animal paw feet with cornucopia brackets. Also found in New York, and probably from the shop of Duncan Phyfe, was the curule form expanded to sofa size.

Another couch at the Museum of Fine Arts in Boston dated 1818 to 1830 and made of rosewood and rosewood graining on birch and maple illustrates a typical Empire couch form. A square base stands on thick fluted legs and brass casters. A silk cushion rests on the base and is met at one end by a small upholstered foot rest. The other end moves into a gracefully scrolled back and side, the flow of which forms a *tête à tête* with the rectangular base.

Thin but effective brass stringing accentuates these forms, making the contrast between straight and curved surfaces more dramatic. Most emphatic on this couch is the stylized brass inlay strategically placed to play off the dark rosewood surface.

New York and Baltimore produced the most decoratively ornate sofas in the Empire style. A New York Grecian sofa made about 1820 and part of New York's Metropolitan Museum of Art collection lacks no decorative detail. Known as the "dolphin sofa" for the legs and scrolled arms that form its body, the sofa is a masterfully balanced composition between sweeping curves and stimulating textural ornament.

The form was shown in the 1802 edition of *The London Chair-Makers' and Carvers' Book of Prices for Workmanship* but the selection of motifs derives from its New York origins. Made from mahogany, the front rail is inset with a brass Greek key or fret, a classical pattern made up of square hooked forms that repeat to create a band.

Brass rosettes punctuate the scrolled ends of the back. Carved and gilded leaf sprays act as brackets that allow the eyes to make a transition from the vertical dolphin legs to the horizontal rail and sweeping back.

Small gold tacks follow the upholstery along every inch of the sofa adding subtle highlights and reinforcement for the form. The dolphins add immense appeal since they are so well integrated with the body; the strongest statement they make is a decorative one.

Carved scales were highlighted with *verde antique,* a green-based paint process that simulated antique bronze. The dolphins add a textural excitement that helps establish this piece as a sophisticated seating object. This sofa is a clever orchestration of form, texture, and ornament.

The Baltimore Empire sofa was typically constructed with a scrolled crest rail, occasionally with rosette terminals. Cornucopia arms, animal paw legs with cornucopia brackets, and rounded seat rails were additional ingredients that helped define the form. Carving was broad yet slightly flat. Baltimore sofas still wearing their original painted decoration are very rare.

Many Empire pieces with broad proportions, swollen forms, and large scale carving have been nicknamed "fat classical." Empire sofas from about 1825 to 1840 as a form live up to this title best.

OPPOSITE PAGE: *While still exhibiting traits associated with the klismos form, this mahogany side chair from Boston begins to show some of the fullness that seating would assume toward the end of the Empire period.* **BELOW:** *In the nineteenth century, couches were often made in pairs to meet the Neoclassical emphasis on symmetrical room arrangement.*

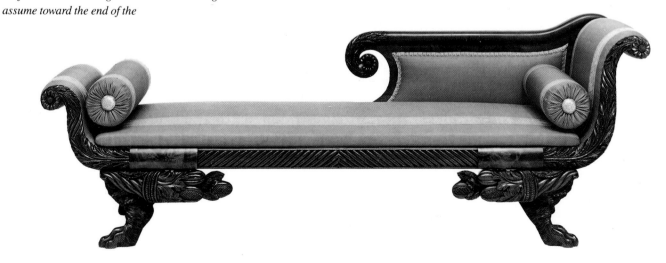

Tables

This New York pier table with winged female caryatid supports by Charles-Honoré Lannuier was made for the brother of Napoleon, Joseph Bonaparte, for his "Point Breeze" estate in New Jersey.

Another group of table forms became fashionable in the Empire period. The center, sofa, and pier tables joined the work, card, and drop-leaf tables in representing the major forms.

The center table drew inspiration from pedestal tables (with tops supported by columns) that were discovered in ancient Rome. These forms were modernized and adapted to the best parlor of the nineteenth-century home.

One favored model was built with three pillars that connect the base to the round top. Besides growing in size from tables of earlier Federal definition, the ornament changed; details were applied with a heavier hand. Gilt acanthus leaves, anthemion, and brass ormolu mounts replace delicate wood inlay.

A center table of this type is illustrated in Henry Sargent's painting *The Tea Party* (c.1821–1825), at the Museum of Fine Arts in Boston. The picture provides documentation of nineteenth-century material culture and records patterns of usage that cannot necessarily be gleaned simply from viewing such an object. The Walters Art Gallery in Baltimore houses the marble-top pedestal that was made in Boston for the artist.

The sofa table, as the name implies, was used in conjunction with the sofa. With little variation, period descriptions, such as those found in Sheraton's *Cabinet Dictionary,* allude to the form as approximately five to six feet (150 to 180 cm) in length with leaves at each end and two drawers that divide the frame in half.

With the exception of the top, many bases mimicked those found on card tables. Possible base configurations include leaf-carved colonnettes and eagle supports resting on animal paw feet with ormolu mounts and gilding.

Found in several areas, including Philadelphia, the form proliferated in New York. Although Duncan Phyfe and Charles-Honoré Lannuier produced some of the most spectacular examples, their blueprints invited duplication by a host of other firms.

The best sofa tables have a form that unites all components, a decorative scheme that brightens but doesn't outshine the facade of the piece, and carving that adds depth. A sofa table with a base of intersecting lyres shows how the form endeared itself to Philadelphians.

The lyre shape has been attributed to Phyfe with more frequency than he deserves. It has been documented as appearing as early as 1794 in Philadelphia. Boston and Baltimore goods also possessed the lyre motif.

New York card tables made by Lannuier displayed the decorative nuances of French taste as spelled out in Pierre de la Mésangère's *Collection des Meubles et Objets de Goût* on characteristically American forms. It is believed that less than one dozen of the Lannuier-labeled or firmly attributed card tables remain.

One group of New York card tables shares certain traits, including the French-inspired caryatid winged figure that supports the top. The common features include the four-footed animal legs that have been painted with *verde antique* to simulate bronze, and acanthus knees.

Discreet differences appear in details, such as the shape and amount of gilt and ormolu. Adding spark are fine finishing quirks, including inlaid brass borders, and surfaces that combine with a symmetrical arrangement.

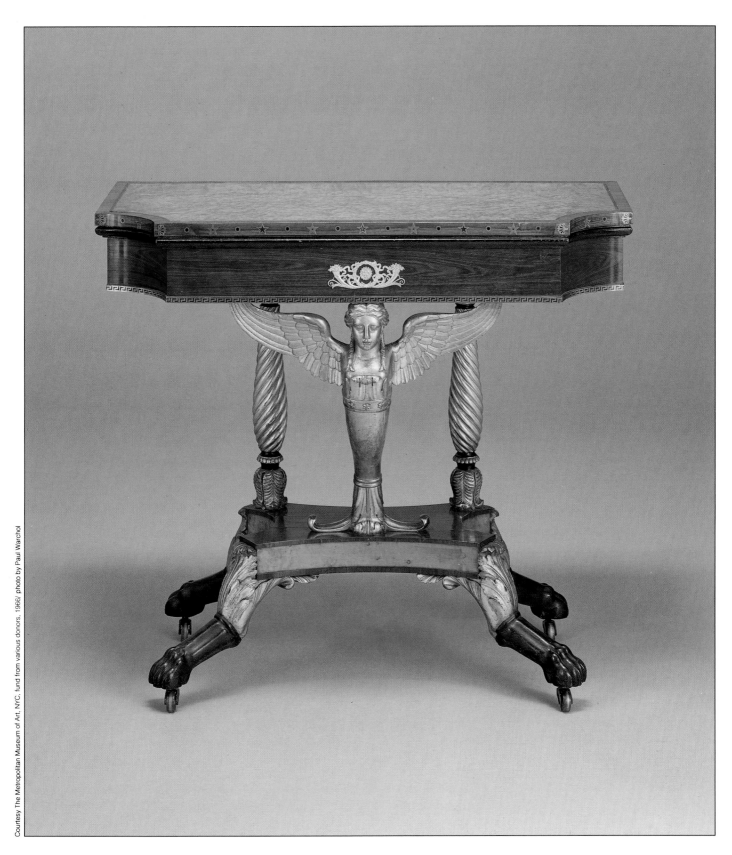

Courtesy The Metropolitan Museum of Art, NYC, fund from various donors, 1966/ photo by Paul Warchol

*This Lannuier-ascribed table once belonged to Philip Hone, former
mayor of New York. The winged figure and carved verde antique
animal paws with leafy hocks were elements that Lannuier adapted
from the French Empire blueprint for his American consumers.*

Even without the benefit of a label, such finely tuned versions point conclusively to the hand of a master artist. Today they are highly sought for their beauty of design and quality of workmanship. Lannuier tables such as these have been found with significant histories in many different regions, indicating the master craftsman's far reaching reputation.

A lesser version following the same design imperatives but executed by a less skillful hand than Lannuier's uses similar details but often at the expense of élan. Gold leaf stencilling and quillwork with gold paint, for example, substitute for the expensive imported French ormolu mounts found on Lannuier's work.

The Baltimore card table is easily recognized by a thick shaft that connects the top to the base of multiple turnings and by its distinct X-frame pedestal base. The cold angularity of the base is warmed with Grecian scrolls or volutes with anthemion and rosettes that have undergone painting, gilding, and the application of brass mounts.

Many were made from pine that had been painted to simulate rosewood. These tables continue an earlier Baltimore tradition in fancy painted furniture. Those of the highest quality are usually attributed to John Finlay, whose reputation for this type of decoration was established in the Federal era.

An enduring form in Europe that was introduced to America in the late eighteenth century was the pier table, which came to be associated with the Empire period.

Originally conceived as a table designed to stand against the pier or wall between two windows or doors, the pier table added a finishing element to the decorative scheme of a balanced room.

Many pier tables followed a single format—square top supported by pillars. Thus, it was the materials, rather than the form, that differentiated them. American pier tables were made with mirrored backs that created a degree of space enhancement. The mirrored backs also added continuity of design with the large pier glass that often hung above the table.

Philadelphia cabinetmakers showed a fondness for richly veined marble and gilt tops and pillars. Boston examples, conversely, relied on mahogany veneers and restrained ormolu mounts.

Baltimore examples often had four free-standing legs with no platform base, or they had a low rectangular base with projecting blocks where the pillar met the base. Legs on these models might have heavy reeding and terminate in block-and-ball feet. Plain surfaces with contrasting veneers added variety to those fancy painted Empire tables with X-shaped bases.

ABOVE LEFT: *The choice of materials and crafting on this ebonized rosewood pier table qualify it as a superlative example of the fully developed New York Empire style.*
BELOW: *Plain stretches of mahogany veneer and the* carved lotus motif around the top of the base point to a Boston locale, circa 1825 to 1830. The form was a pastiche of the pedestal tables discovered in digs at ancient sites in Rome.

Bedsteads

The high-post bedsteads that were popular from the early eighteenth century onward continued to be made. An Empire innovation was the low-to-the-ground sleigh bed. On this model, the headboard and footboard are the same height, and both parts curve outward in the shape of a sleigh.

The sleigh bedstead is a close relative of a French prototype that was known in France by several names, including the *lit en bateau,* or boat-bed, and the *lit en courbeille,* or basket-bed. The flowing lines of this bed made it ideally suited to the Empire period.

Bonaparte's wife, Josephine, and Madame Récamier both owned bedsteads of this type. They helped to popularize the sleigh form in France and in the hearts of American francophiles.

It was most popular in New York; Lannuier made one for the Van Renselaer family. In the French manner, ormolu was called upon to trim the relatively simple form.

As are most of Lannuier's best pieces, this New York high-post bedstead is fashioned from mahogany. The fluted posts with acanthus carving, the flared head and footboard, and the painted canopy rail with stars and eagles are all believed to be by his hand.

Restauration, or Pillar and Scroll, Style
(1830–1840)

As far as possible, the style of the United States is blended with European taste, and a graceful outline and simplicity of parts are depicted in all the objects.

John Hall, Baltimore cabinetmaker

Compared to the Empire style, which was still considered an outgrowth of Napoleon's "ruling taste," the Restauration style saw the aristocratic component wrung out of furniture design. Indeed, the entire symbolism of furniture had changed.

Up to this point in the realm of cabinetmaking, period furniture design followed mandates laid out by style setters (designers working under the auspices of royalty or the affluent). But by the beginning of the third decade of the nineteenth century, technology brought a wide range of goods to the growing middle class. Annual fairs and exhibits became the vehicles that influenced consumption patterns and goaded industry to even loftier performances.

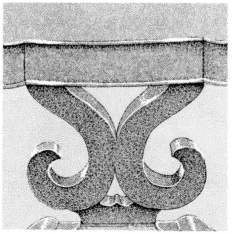

The individual cabinetmaker took a back seat in this scenario.

The culmination of the American nineteenth-century Neoclassical movement is referred to as the Restauration, or Pillar and Scroll, style. By this period, the Neoclassical ideal was fully exploited, and the last stage was short-lived, influencing furniture design over the relatively brief period from the 1830s to 1840s.

While both terms refer to the same style interval, the terms derive from different sources. Restauration refers to the French style of the same name that emerged after the fall of Napoleon, while the term Pillar and Scroll describes the primary visual elements that characterized the style.

Style Overview ✑

The Restauration style was introduced in France about the time of the restoration of the Bourbon monarchy in 1815. In form, objects reverted to a geometric simplicity; plain mahogany or rosewood veneer expanses combined with C- and S-curves that were cut into pillars and scrolls. The curves were square in section.

Just as the Restauration signaled the end of Napoleon's Empire, so, too, did it signal the end of dressy applied ornament. Surfaces were plain but received sculptural mass from the broad application of C- and S-curves. Carving and gilding disappeared entirely.

In the Restauration style, the archaeological character of Empire furniture dissolved into a simplicity of components that were both efficient and economically justifiable. A coarseness of design swept in that at once dissolved the finesse of Federal furniture and buried the archaeological treasures of the Empire.

One benefit was that unadorned furniture could be turned out at a faster pace than highly ornamented work. Less labor-intensive pieces were also less costly and became available to the widest range of consumers since the inception of furniture making. Most households could now afford a sofa, a form which due to its size and costly ornament had traditionally been reserved for the wealthy.

Simultaneously, the introduction of the steam-driven band saw enabled manufacturers to easily and quickly produce the thick scrolls associated with the style. The new invention enabled furniture makers to keep production costs relatively low compared to the previous era's labor-intensive techniques with their many hand-finished details.

Thus, furniture making came to depend less on the skill of the highly specialized individual cabinetmaker and more on a mechanized, mass production process. As the mortise-and-tenon joint heralded the beginning of individualized furniture making, the Industrial Revolution surely marked its demise.

Those responsible for the manufacture of a piece of furniture no longer had contact with the consumer and a long-standing tradition of communication between cabinetmaker and patron was lost. Retailers—often working through catalogues—made the buying process that much less personal.

These developments ultimately led to a succession of

Courtesy The Strong Museum, Rochester, NY

mid-to-late nineteenth-century mass-produced styles which, with few exceptions, were composed of eclectic ingredients borrowed indiscriminately from previous periods. These additive assemblages were superimposed on machine-made bodies.

The Pillar and Scroll style bridged the gap between the handcrafted objects from the past and the completely machine-made examples that emerged after 1840. In the realm of furniture design, it was a brief transition from the Pillar and Scroll style, which incorporated technology to the later styles that were totally dependent on it.

When looking at furniture from the years approaching 1840, it is more important to recognize forms than it is to pick out the hand of a specific cabinetmaker or regional school. John Hall's *The Cabinet Maker's Assistant* (1840), the first American pattern book, introduced the rudiments of the Pillar and Scroll style to the widest group of furniture makers. Like his revered predecessors such as Chippendale, Hepplewhite, and Sheraton, English immigrant Hall codified the style, citing the elliptical curve as the most beautiful of all design elements. His illustrations helped the style spread from Baltimore to Boston, New Orleans, and as far west as the Mississippi.

ABOVE: *The design of this Pillar and Scroll parlor set is completely dominated by the elliptical curve. The gondola chair and the* méridienne, *or lounging sofa of asymmetrical form, were period innovations.*
OPPOSITE PAGE: *This lozenge-shaped center table with marble top is attributed to John Hall. The scroll supports identify it as late classical.*

For the first time, expression of regional differences became less important; stocking adequate inventories and the new fascination of subtleties in marketing outweighed perceived differences in design—hundreds of firms across America were capable of manufacturing the Pillar and Scroll style.

As increased mechanization made the style readily available to the middle-class, America took the lead in producing pattern books, thus further expanding the market. The Pillar and Scroll style was the ultimate expression of mid-nineteenth century American self-direction.

The style flourished around the country but New York took the lead in embracing the plain surface, scroll supports, and columns characteristic of the style. The workshop of Joseph Meeks & Sons (active 1797–1868), a Phyfe competitor, initially gained repute during the Empire period. Cabinetmakers were quick to sense changes in taste and in technology. Indeed, their survival depended on it.

Phyfe's shop, long known for its Federal and Empire furniture of the highest style and quality, followed this trend as well. In 1837, Phyfe produced a fourteen piece suite of parlor furniture in the Restauration format for a prominent New York lawyer, Samuel A. Foote.

A lithograph printed in 1833 illustrated more than forty pieces in the Pillar and Scroll style available through Joseph Meeks & Sons. As with many large-scale furniture operations, agents located in other cities increased the firm's visibility and sales.

OPPOSITE PAGE: *A large assortment of heavy, plain furniture that made up the opus of Restauration, or Pillar and Scroll, furniture is advertized in a broadside by Joseph Meeks & Sons in 1833.* **ABOVE:** *The extremely plain style of this wardrobe predominated throughout America in the Restauration, or last phase of Neoclassicism, and in some areas, even longer.* **LEFT:** *The beading around the inset panels on this commode add emphasis to an otherwise plain form.*

Case Pieces

A

ntoine-Gabriel Quervelle (1789–1856), a Paris-
born cabinetmaker active in Philadelphia,
worked in both the Empire and Pillar and Scroll
styles. His early designs, most notably a secretary-
bookcase, won him a silver medal in the 1827 exhibition
sponsored by The Franklin Institute of the State of Pennsylvania. The piece is labelled in five places.

The humongous mahogany cabinet recalls the highly
decorative Meeks secretary from New York. Although
lacking the decorative stencilled painting of the Meeks
example, there are plenty of details to amuse the eye. The
piece was built with a protruding cornice, columns, and
animal paw feet.

A large lunette of veneered mahogany panels and
simple carving portend the approaching simplicity of the
Restauration style. Baccarat drawer pulls and almost
indiscernible ormolu mounts supply the only applied
ornament. The Quervelle secretary can be seen at the
Philadelphia Museum of Art.

Quervelle's later work and that of his contemporaries
followed the Pillar and Scroll edict, with a limited array
of choices of forms. There are several reasons why this
happened. Regionalism and hand crafting were no longer
the most significant elements of furniture design; further,
increased communication spread the style rapidly and
with greater accuracy.

Increased shipping to other cities within the states led to
more uniform interpretations. Previously, cabinetmakers
often had to recreate pieces from memory of work they had
seen somewhere else. The variations that emerged were valued. By the 1830s, however, many cabinetmakers advertised that they could "execute orders from any part of the
Union." Objects were readily available for the copying.

ABOVE RIGHT: *A large lunette of veneered mahogany panels and
simple carving on this huge secretary portend the simplicity of the
Restauration style. It won Philadelphian Antoine-Gabriel Quervelle a
silver medal in an 1827 exhibition.* **OPPOSITE PAGE, TOP:** *An
upholstered armchair with a tall, rolled back was often referred to as
a Voltaire chair, because the poet was depicted seated in such a chair.*
OPPOSITE, BOTTOM: *The balanced arrangement of these stools
takes precedent over any superfluous ornament and records the
progression of Empire style into the simpler Pillar and Scroll format.*

Courtesy Philadelphia Museum of Art, gift of Mr. & Mrs. Edward C. Page in memory of Robert E. Griffith

Seating ✐

Chairs of the Restauration were predominantly of the gondola type, so named for the boat-back or French *chair en gondole,* which gently curved around the back. The gondola chair has a downward curving back that forms supports for the arms. The back is open and has a solid and wide back splat.

The sofa kept the large scale that served it well in the Empire period but it dismissed archaeological associations in favor of plain, contoured surfaces and scroll supports. The Restauration sofa had a high scrolled back with a single expanse of mahogany for the crest rail.

It also had scrolled arms, a swelled front rail, and large S-scroll supports for legs. The Lyman Allyn Museum located in New London, Connecticut, holds a sofa of this particular type.

Another Restauration seating form was the méridienne, a short sofa with one arm higher than the other. Some upholstery patterns were large and symmetrical, with the symmetricality the only quality held over from the earlier stages of Neoclassicism. Upholstery began to take on some of the plumpness it would assume by mid-century.

Tables ✺

Tables were broad expanses of straight lines juxtaposed with scrolls arranged in a variety of ways, albeit with heavy proportions. The arrangement of these scrolls often presented the only degree of differentiation between models.

With the exception of pier tables, most tables had four scrolled legs. Thinly applied mahogany or rosewood veneers were affixed to the body and made for a rich but quiet surface. Marble tops provided some contrast.

Large case pieces exhibited some proclivity for broad veneered surfaces and scroll supports. Smaller pieces such as the server were occasionally raised on rectangular legs with turnings above the block and below it.

A scrolled back piece similar to what might be found on a sofa acted as a backboard on some cases. Pressed glass drawer pulls were a radical departure from the brass and ormolu mounts of the past. The glass pulls became almost synonymous with late Neoclassicism.

Since so many Pillar and Scroll pieces were made throughout America using the same forms, it is difficult without the aid of labels or strong provenances to document much Restauration furniture with certainty to a regional area. Characteristics that were once the exclusive hallmark of the cabinetmaker became displaced or disguised by the impersonal band saw. Descriptions, therefore, are looser than those found on eighteenth-century items.

Courtesy Ronald Bourgeault, Hampton, MA/photo by Joyce Golden & Associates, Inc., NYC

Bedsteads

By the nineteenth century, bedsteads endorsed a more modern idea, moving away from the concept of an upholstered "room inside a room," which dominated the majority of sleeping forms for centuries. Following the lead established by Empire designs, upholstered, self-contained forms were often discarded in favor of the sleigh bedstead.

Opposed to earlier convention where a bedstead was placed with its head against a wall, the sleigh bedstead was often set with its side against the wall. This practice followed the lead of French prototypes.

The Restauration bedstead was a sleigh form stripped of its classical ornament. The high-post bedstead as a form continued to be made but it differed measurably from those that preceded it. Characteristic of the late Neoclassical era, the form had swelled and was topped with a heavy cornice and a high headboard.

OPPOSITE PAGE: Marble tops often provided relief from expansive wood-grained surfaces on Pillar and Scroll forms. Characteristics that were once the thumbprint of a particular artisan disappeared in favor of quickly assembled objects available to a wider range of buyers. **BELOW:** *The sleigh bedstead was based on a popular French model known by several names, the* lit en bateau *(boat-bed), or the* lit en courbeille *(basket-bed). Painted versions carried the form into mid-century and became part of country home furnishings called "cottage furniture."*

The pieces of furniture in this room are reproductions, not original antiques—the sofa, for instance, is copied from an American Empire sofa in the collection of the Smithsonian Institution. Reproductions are line-for-line, detail-for-detail copies of original antique pieces. They are often the ideal purchase for individuals who would like to own a particular antique but cannot possibly afford it.

Part III ✦ Connoisseurship and Collecting

A Word To The Wise

Among mortals, second thoughts are wisest.

Euripides

A growing cadre of collectors interested in American antique furniture combined with a scarcity of pieces can spell danger for the uninformed. Consequently, it behooves collectors—those just starting as well as those more seasoned—to educate and refine the eyes before reaching for the wallet. A healthy dose of skepticism will also help to ease one past the emotional euphoria and love-at-first-sight stage toward the rational, decision-making stage.

Molière cautioned that "one is easily fooled by that which one loves." Unfortunately, many antique aficionados never make it past the emotion of the first stage.

Buyer's remorse hurts whatever the price tag. And the old adage that a fool and his money are soon parted holds true notably on the purchase side of a mistake; mistakes are harder to dispose of, especially in a market that has grown measurably savvy.

Scholarship and the refinements of connoisseurship will give the collector an understanding of what makes an object a mediocre example of its kind and what makes it a truly outstanding one.

Such knowledge will also prove an invaluable ally when assessing the genuineness of the article and how the marketplace rewards this originality of design.

The following are suggested as some general guidelines for collecting that have proven helpful to scholars, collectors, dealers, and others devoted to the American decorative arts. Space in this text does not permit a lengthy perusal of each point, so would-be collectors are encouraged to explore this discourse in greater detail through the sources listed in the bibliography or through the services of a competent advisor. Myrna Kaye's book, *Fake, Fraud, or Genuine,* is an excellent source of elucidation for many of the points discussed here.

This cupboard typifies the remade object. Old parts were skinned of their finish, and new parts, including the top, turnings, and dentil molding, were later enhancements. The application of paint was streaked with black paint to simulate age.

Connoisseurship ✺

Try to determine a main area of collecting or scholarly interest. Such a focus will keep the collection coherent and it works whether one is building an entire collection or looking for a single item. Nevertheless, it is a good idea to avoid becoming too rigid in scope, for some of the best collections often mix objects from different regions or from slightly different stylistic intervals for their beauty and originality of design. This indeed mimics period practice; objects were much too dear to be whimsically cast off with each approaching fashion.

The would-be collector should become thoroughly familiar with the style in which he or she is interested. For an understanding of any style, it is necessary to become conversant with its macro features, or those features associated with all objects from that time frame. The main points to know are: dates; underlying form, components, and scale; materials; and ornament, including hardware, carving, inlay, veneering, and paint.

More advanced collectors who have these concepts firmly in mind will benefit from familiarizing themselves with certain micro features, or those occurring in a more narrowly defined universe. They include regional characteristics (claw-and-ball feet from specific geographic regions, for example) and names of cabinetmakers associated with that style. An advanced collector may also wish to become knowledgeable about the origins of the style.

Except for imported woods such as mahogany, most cabinetmakers relied on locally supplied woods. It helps to know what primary and secondary woods were used in a particular region. These micro features have of late played a larger role in the understanding of American antiques.

Beyond scholarly material in texts, view as many objects as possible first-hand. In addition to museums and historical societies, antique shows, and auction houses provide some advantages that most public institutions do not.

A good dealer can become a trusted ally in the pursuit of American treasures from the past; on the other hand, an unscrupulous dealer can lure an unsuspecting purchaser into a trap baited with fakes and frauds. While the activities of the dishonest purveyor cannot be listed here singly, those of the reputable dealer can.

Above-board dealers will provide the purchaser with adequate time to authenticate the piece, perhaps several days to a week. And those proprietors who allow the object to be viewed on loan (within reason) prior to final sale often establish the best dealer/collector rapport. This strategy applies only to those objects that have passed preliminary scrutiny.

Some of the same safeguards apply to buying through dealers who dominate the trade in general. A dealer should be able to intelligently answer questions relating to the item. After all, most dealers have their own capital tied up in the inventory. If they are at all reticent about sharing information, one might wonder what potential problems they are concealing. Sometimes that which says the most is that which is left unsaid.

All important information relating to the work should be verifiable, be in writing on the bill of sale, and come with a return privilege should the object not check out in terms of its period legitimacy, provenance, or any other feature upon which the purchaser would likely act.

Auction previews, when objects scheduled for sale are exhibited prior to the event, provide another excellent learning forum. All items can be examined and handled by the public without obligation.

Potential auction bidders are encouraged to do some careful sleuthing. It isn't at all uncommon to see potential bidders, whether they be scholars, collectors, or dealers, turning over chairs, removing drawers, taking measurements, or engaging in other activities destined to reveal a potential treasure or unmask a fraud. Those individuals who go to a preview with a goal make the most productive use of their time.

Anyone wishing to learn more about a piece up for auction, including its provenance or history, condition, and so on should check with the auction house to determine if a "condition report" is available. Most auction houses will share this information with potential bidders as a courtesy. Larger firms usually have department specialists available to answer specific questions.

Potential bidders are cautioned, however, to remember that *caveat emptor*—"let the buyer beware"—is the watchword for auction buying. Most objects are sold on an "as is" basis. Check the auction catalogue for the rules governing the auction as they differ from state to state and from one firm to another.

This chest shows signs of being forged. The sides are old drawer fronts that have been plugged, and the top and back are from another chest. The blocking on the base has been added from another source. The very appearance of a "rare" nine-shell case is cause for alarm.

Long before reaching for an auction paddle, a discerning collector will get comfortable with auction proceedings. Would-be collectors can begin by attending several sales without any intent to buy, just to get a feel for the mechanics of the event. Never feel pressured by the time constraints of the auction process. Never rely solely on the description in the catalogue as truth.

Needless to say, few collectors have pockets deep enough to ante up multi-million dollar sums for a documented eighteenth-century Newport secretary desk. A collector should, however, buy the best example he or she can find and afford.

It is imperative that the collector buy originality of design and quality of form and execution. He or she should not be cajoled into buying antique furniture strictly for "investment purposes." The American decorative arts marketplace—as sophisticated as it has become—still depends on extraneous, immeasurable variables including matters of personal taste.

This marketplace is also subject to some of the same economic ebbs and flows that influence disposable income. It would be the wisest individual of all who could predict with accuracy the timing and direction of these shifts. Unlike stocks, bonds, or other financial investments, antiques, or real assets, do not lend themselves well to the financial equations that so dominate the capital markets.

Due to the soaring values of period furniture and the potential for fraudulent activity that is a by-product of these soaring prices, collectors must also assess furniture for its period legitimacy. The ultimate goal is to distinguish the acceptable imperfections found on all genuine antique pieces from those with excessive restoration or enhancement.

Authenticity ᥱᢀᢀ

Greedy miscreants wishing to fill the void left by a dwindling cache of authentic period pieces have profited handsomely from deceptive activities, which fall into two categories, the fake and the fraud.

Fake pieces are complete forgeries. Fraudulent pieces, on the other hand, are genuine antiques that have undergone alteration or enhancement, or have been misrepresented in terms of authorship, provenance, or any detail upon which a purchaser might act.

A sampling of fake and fraudulent practices will underscore the need for caution: complete fakes; new objects fashioned from old parts; remade antiques; enhanced objects or those that have had a "facelift"; married pieces; English or European objects being passed off as American; and reproductions masquerading as the real thing.

Complete fakes are less common than they were fifty to sixty years ago. Today's astute collector recognizes them and the herculean effort necessary to simulate a genuine antique would not be adequately rewarded in today's marketplace. Technology, including microanalysis of materials, has made it much simpler to detect fakes.

This is not to say, however, that fakes haven't found their way into many collections where they may be proudly displayed as genuine. Some institutions, including the Metropolitan Museum of Art, Winterthur, and Yale, have included fakes in their study collections in order to educate viewers to the tricks of the forger.

More prevalent but equally despicable is the practice of passing off as antique a new object fashioned from antique or old parts. Truly old parts make a more believable fake than one created from those that have merely been "antiqued" to simulate age. A common deception is the fashioning of non-furniture forms into furniture. Floors or walls from a barn, for example, might be resurrected as tabletops, facades, or sides for case pieces.

This category also covers the conversion of old forms into rarer, usually costlier, versions. Beware of any piece referred to as a "rare example" or "rare form." This description has caught many collectors bent on pursuing the unique. Remember, even accounting for regional differences in ornament and in construction technique, most period furniture was conceived with some consistency of design: A true rarity is unlikely.

Courtesy The Henry Francis du Pont Winterthur Museum, DE, gift of Mr. James Biddle, April 1963

This Philadelphia Chippendale chair has obvious clues that point to a forgery. The most glaring error is a body made from oak, not mahogany or walnut. The carving is lifeless and the crude claw-and-ball feet scream reproduction.

Remade antiques require slightly less creativity on the part of the unscrupulous. Whereas a new object fashioned from old or antique parts might require some cabinetmaking skills, remade objects often require little such ability.

The remade may be an object given new life by something as simple as separating a two-part high chest so that the lower half can be sold as a dressing table, a piece that fits the scaled down lifestyle of many of today's collectors. The top may then be reborn as a chest of drawers with the addition of feet. Adding elements is another trick; fancy cornices or pediments add drama, elegance, and increased profit to a simpler flat-top high chest.

Closely aligned with remades are enhanced antiques, or those that have had "aesthetic surgery." This category accounts for a large number of problematic antiques. The practice sometimes hinges on trends. For example, when a Philadelphia Chippendale piecrust tea table set a record for the form at auction, lesser examples were undoubtedly endowed with a piecrust edge and rigorous carving.

Carving is one of the prime ways in which old objects are augmented. Shells and fans, features that might change a banal piece into a masterpiece, are common motifs employed in this chicanery. Plain table leaves are often scalloped in an effort to increase their desirability.

Paint can also be used deceptively. Rarely does furniture exist with its original paint. Complicating the investigative process is the fact that many pieces were unpainted originally and then were painted at a later date. Many so-called japanned objects were originally bare, with decorative detail and embellishment supplied later in the nineteenth century.

To a practiced eye, these pieces usually reveal themselves as incongruous in much the same manner as the somewhat lifeless carving found in late nineteenth-century work. On other less complicated painted surfaces the appearance of paint in nicks and gouged areas suggests that the paint and the surface to which it was applied did not join forces at the same time.

Later inlay embellishment, a trick especially common on Federal or early Neoclassical compositions, joins re-veneering as a technique that can render an otherwise authentic piece an orphan. While honest small repairs are acceptable, fraudulent tampering is most unwelcome.

As surely as cheap watches and leather goods sold by street vendors lure status seekers bent on designer labels, fake furniture labels and inscriptions are designed to fool an audience hooked on a designer label of another kind. Many a collector has been duped by this practice.

With married objects, fakers use two disparate pieces to create one saleable antique. For example, the upper half of a high chest often gets estranged from its base, which may be cavorting in the market as a remade dressing table. Consequently, a suitable partner must be found for the upper chest. When it is, the new piece is passed off to unknowledgeable purchasers. This is the opposite of what fakers do with remades, when one antique is split up to do double duty as two. Again, high chests, desks, and bookcases are prime targets. Getting familiar with certain dimensions of scale can aid the viewer in spotting these rogues.

The stylistic influence on much American antique furniture is conclusively English. Some provincial English furniture, therefore, may pass as American. A sad progression finds certain purveyors acquiring less costly English pieces with the intent of passing them off to naive consumers as their costlier American cousins.

As the saying goes, imitation is the sincerest form of flattery. Many reproductions started life as tributes to the originality of design and craftsmanship that marked the period piece. Some are fairly accurate copies; others are more loosely adapted pastiches.

Most reproductions have been constructed using contemporary techniques and tools. The intent is not to deceive but to mimic a particular style. Such reproductions are distinct from outright fakes that are expressly meant to deceive, employing what at first glance appear to be period construction techniques and materials.

To a trained eye and hand there are, however, subtle differences in design, proportion, or ornament that yield clues as to period authenticity. Blatant mixing of regional attributes is a dead giveaway of the non-authentic item. Philadelphia Chippendale carving found on a bombé form from Boston, for example, has the main features of the Rococo style but shows total disregard for the regional traits of the style by mixing it with a typically Boston form.

A reproduction is not a problem when the purchaser knows what he or she is buying. The danger with reproductions comes when a dishonest seller falsely representing the object as of the period is matched with an untrained and uninformed purchaser who misses the inaccuracies of style, and believes the piece to be genuine.

Collectors should learn some commonly used terminology that helps to differentiate true period pieces from revivals or reproductions. Aboveboard dealers and auction houses will classify furniture as to avoid confusion. A chair, for example, may be described in several different ways.

An American Chippendale chair might be described as "Philadelphia Chippendale chair, circa 1770." This tells the viewer that the chair is of the period and describes its regional attribution. A similar-looking chair might be described as "Chippendale chair, nineteenth century," or as "Chippendale centennial chair."

This chair, however, has quite a different history. In the mid- to late-nineteenth century, many styles from the past were reproduced. Known in the trade as "centennials," many of these objects made their debut roughly one hundred years after the original style. (1876 was a popular year for centennials in all media that immortalized America's one hundred year history.) In furniture, centennials are often close renderings of the authentic period piece, some with nearly identical attributes.

Centennials have "some age" but their status and value in the marketplace are diminished. The originality of design that marked the period arrangement is not manifested in the centennial and its price should reflect this difference. With practice, centennials become readily distinguishable from their period prototypes. ;

The description "centennial" or "nineteenth century" clearly distinguishes this chair from the period chair. Thus, even if a collector is not fully familiar with the visual evidence, knowledge of the terminology will help to classify the piece. Those who get tripped up by centennials often do not have the fundamentals of the style (in this case its dates) firmly committed to memory.

The words "nineteenth century" should instantly trip an alarm in the potential buyer's mind that a chair from this time frame was not made during the years from 1755 to 1790, the reign of the Chippendale style. Centennial descriptions are less specific than those found on original period objects, and some tradespeople don't make any differentiations, leaving it to the purchaser to understand the difference.

The most popular and enduring styles have been reproduced for years, and many are still copied today. A reproduction chair of this sort shares the visual attributes of the original stylistic interval but it is not an antique. This category of chair can be as new as one that might be found at a local furniture store. Its primary value is decorative. An accurate description for such a reproduction chair might read "Chippendale-style chair," with style, not age, being the key word.

A word of caution: Label-hungry collectors have been led astray by attaching too much importance to one feature even when other components within the same piece present conflicting evidence. Never accept a description as doctrine, no matter what the source. Deceptions aside, dealers, museums, and auction houses occasionally err in the cataloguing process. Unlike the American judicial system, in the realm of antique furniture, each piece should be "guilty until proven innocent."

How, then, is a collector to avoid the pitfalls of fakes and frauds? Connoisseurship—knowledge and experience— is the collector's best ally in the war against counterfeits. Serious scholars and collectors are completely familiar with all of the ingredients of a style, both general and regional. (Or, they have an expert advisor.)

Collectors can also develop a checklist of object-specific evidentiary properties that will become as well known to them as the style checklist in protecting against deception. These include: economy of labor and consistency of construction; identification rules governing labels and period attributions; personalized inscriptions; and technology.

Economy of labor, discussed throughout this text, acknowledges the opportunity cost of the cabinetmaker's time. Also worth repeating: Effort would not be expended where it would not show. On a case piece a cabinetmaker would not, for example, stain, varnish, or smooth certain parts of the interior that were obstructed from view or that did not have contact with any of its contents.

Time spent on such unnecessary work would detract from other activities in which the cabinetmaker might otherwise be productively engaged. The appearance of stain or excessive finishing in such an area should surely raise a red flag in the mind of the sleuth.

Economy of labor was closely linked with economy of materials. The best woods were used judiciously and only where their presence would be immediately noticed. With a few notable exceptions, costly mahogany would be used for veneering surfaces while a secondary wood such as pine would be a likely choice for frames or drawers.

While it would be unusual to find a knot on the surface of a high style piece, economy of material might justify the inclusion of a knot on an area that was not visible. It was also not unheard of for a period cabinetmaker to have occasionally incorporated an odd piece of scrap wood into a drawer bottom. This should not be cause for alarm if all other evidence supports period construction.

Those with less-than-honest intentions often contradict such utilitarian practices. They expend more effort and materials "antiquing" objects. Such fraudulent activity might show up as a varnished or painted surface or a too smooth finish on an unexposed area.

Consistency of workmanship is another quality to be considered. Regardless of whether one is analyzing a seventeenth-century piece or a later product of the specialized cabinetmaking shops, consistency of workmanship prevailed. Dovetails or methods of joinery should be similar throughout the piece. Specifically, dovetails on drawers should match, from the top drawers to those on the bottom. Variations in joinery might signal a marriage of parts.

Besides dovetails, tool marks and general assembly procedures can proffer clues as to authenticity. Totally

This high chest from the Housatonic River Valley of Connecticut has been enhanced through the addition of an extra *carved shell on the upper case. On close inspection, plugged holes suggest the drawer originally had a handle.*

glass-like drawer bottoms on an eighteenth-century form, for example, don't equate with period practice. And circular saw marks (found honestly on late nineteenth-century work) are another giveaway that something is amiss; many early pieces retain telltale linear planing marks.

Again, economy of labor did not dictate their removal since they would not be visible. Anyone assuming that such plane marks should have been totally smoothed away is operating under the influence of late nineteenth-century technology-accustomed sensibilities.

Most inconsistencies of labor and materials will become obvious if the interested party continues to ask "does this make sense given the object's purported period?" The best scholars and collectors continue to mentally challenge their skills by asking this question.

Identifiers such as labels and inscriptions are both a blessing and a curse. In a label-hungry market, their presence can add a degree of personalization by the maker, increasing desirability and cost along the way. On the downside, their appearance should instantly alert the

collector to a possible pitfall, for they are another variable that must be authenticated separately from the object to which they are affixed.

Some common problems with labels include the later addition of altered stationery or billheads. Billheads are similar to current-day invoices; they are often dated. Unlike billheads, labels usually have decorative borders all around and are not dated. One way to determine whether the label and the object started life together is to examine the label and the area to which it has been affixed for signs of age.

Most period labels have experienced a degree of loss. Paper yellows and glue dries and gets brittle. Common sense dictates that if the label looks too perfect, especially around the edges, it probably is too perfect to be real.

The wood beneath the label should look different than the wood that has been exposed to air. The covered portion will have experienced less oxidation and will be lighter in color than the remainder of the wood.

This rule holds true for all areas that have had differing degrees of exposure to air, regardless of whether the object is labelled. Unvarnished drawer sides, for example, are darker in front where air, debris, and the oil from owners' hands all combine to darken the front. The rear part of the drawer, on the other hand, would have been subject to less handling and experienced less exposure to air. This accounts for the graduated color on the true period drawer side.

Labels that state a name and perhaps an address with no other identifiers can be further cause for suspicion. Many a collector has been lulled into accepting a label only to find out at a later date that the individual whose label it is was never engaged in the cabinetmaking trade.

City directories, newspapers, and town public records can often confirm or deny a hunch. Many historical societies have published lists of known cabinetmakers and will readily share this information with the public.

Beware of inscriptions. While they are coveted for bringing one closer to the spirit of the maker, they may not be by the hand of the maker. Rather, they may have been done much later to enhance a piece. Separately, owners often inscribed furniture, as have other craftspeople, including those who may have restored or repaired the piece at a later date. A careful collector will assess each of these possibilities and their potential impact on the object's desirability.

Another form of documentation relates to an antique's provenance, or history of ownership. Bills of sale that are ambiguous or incomplete can be problematical documentation. A bill that generically describes tables or chairs could describe virtually any table or chair in a household from a Pilgrim era turned chair to a Neoclassical chair. Genuine bills of sale can be beneficial in helping to lock in a location or possible date of manufacture.

Conversely, a bill of sale is a favorite way to give status to an otherwise unnoteworthy work. A bill of sale can be genuine, genuine to the period but not related to the object in question, or totally fake. Unless the bill can be documented to a specific piece with a high degree of certainty it should be cause for alarm, or cause for further research at the very least.

Verbal provenances can present their own set of problems. Far too many individuals have placed faith in verbal histories or attributions. There are some objects circulating that have mysteriously acquired incorrect lineage due to negligence or deception.

As with printed descriptions, never assume that a verbal history is entirely accurate. Many deceitful individuals count on verbal inaccuracies since they are sometimes more difficult to pin down. And it is far easier to deny or separate oneself from a false word-of-mouth statement should a problem arise.

Further, don't assume that since an object is from a public institution or prominent collection that it is what it alleges to be. Museums deaccess collections for reasons beyond the standard of raising funds for new acquisitions or because they don't conform with an acknowledged collecting focus. They also sell their mistakes.

Separately, science and technology provide another layer of object-specific evidence that can either confirm or deny the authenticity of the object in question. Recall that the irregularly shaped rose-headed or hand-forged nails were used consistently until the dawn of the nineteenth century. So, cut nails found in objects supposedly dating before 1790 are cause for misgiving. And wire and round-headed nails didn't make their appearance until the last quarter of the nineteenth century.

Old wrought nails do not alone confirm period authenticity as they can be salvaged and reused. More importantly, however, they can be examined to establish whether the wrought nail has been in place for an extended length of time.

Corroding wrought iron (ferrous oxide) blackens the wood surrounding the area in which it has been secured. Due to warping and shrinkage of the wood, many of these fasteners are no longer flush with the surface.

Technological innovations such as the X-ray have long assisted the medical community in diagnosing potential problems. Their usefulness in the decorative arts is a more recent phenomena but is well known to many scholars in the field.

X-rays have, for example, revealed hidden, modern, round dowel joints that replaced the older, stronger mortise-and-tenon joint. Modern machine-made dowels signify at the very least a repair, if not a much later work in its entirety.

Black or ultraviolet light has been used successfully in the fine arts to separate later applications of paint to an original surface. Later additions of paint fluoresce differently, often revealing telltale black patches where restoration has occurred.

Ultraviolet lights can prove helpful in spotting discrepancies with painted furniture, too. This infrequently employed technique, as well as that of the X-ray, should be reserved for special cases that remain puzzling only after exhaustion of the aforementioned methods of authentication.

The science of wood, including its species, how it ages and warps, and other inherent qualities such as hardness or softness, is lengthy enough to warrant its own chapter. Suffice it to say, however, that the ability to recognize the most commonly used primary and secondary woods is a most useful tool for the would-be collector.

Microanalysis of woods, whereby a small sliver of wood running with the grain is analyzed to determine its species and place of origin, has added another degree of confidence to many scholarly attributions. This technological innovation has recently served to help recategorize some American antique furniture. Unlike X-rays, microanalysis is available to a wider audience through many state agricultural offices or extensions.

Courtesy Historic Deerfield, Inc., MA/photo by Amanda Merullo

OPPOSITE PAGE: *This chest with drawer is a pastiche that recalls the sunflower chest from Wethersfield, Connecticut. It is a reproduction, not a fake or a fraud. Made about 1900, it has modern construction techniques that were not practiced in Pilgrim-era work.*

ABOVE: *Perhaps the most well-documented fake, this Brewster chair was modelled after one at Pilgrim Hall in Plymouth, Massachusetts. It took its maker more than two months to fake a three-hundred-year-old chair.*

As has been discussed, unfinished wood darkens with age. Secondary woods need to be examined for the mellow color that they acquire with hundreds of years of service. Surfaces closest to the source of air will darken more. Each part should be analyzed in relation to its source of air.

Use common sense to determine the color changes found on the object. The artificially aged color acquired by the application of stain, coffee, or tea is frequently too uniform and opaque in consistency. Untreated wood darkens when exposed to air but it remains clear. It doesn't take on the cloudy appearance that can be found on many faked pieces.

Another word about finishes. Most antiques no longer sport their original finishes. Some pieces were stripped to within an inch of their lives, taking away years of patina,

or matured, encrusted coloring, when the fashion was for antiques to look perfect. Most of this type of activity occurred earlier in the twentieth century when the value of the patina was not yet recognized. It occasionally happens today in the hands of an incompetent restorer.

Collectors and others in the know have long eschewed this practice, and favor pieces with more conservative refinishing that leaves some of the rich patina supplied by years of wear and wax. The personality of the finish remains. Collectors are encouraged to obtain the services of a competent restorer should they contemplate any changes to a finish.

Furniture with a glaringly high-gloss finish is a poor second to an old, carefully executed refinish or to a new finish that has shown respect for the history of the object. Historical societies, dealers, and museums are often a good source of names for quality restorers.

Technology-driven analysis is not always necessary; indeed, the curious collector can use his or her eyes, ears, and hands to good effect when investigating a possible treasure from the past.

All antiques, no matter how lovingly they have been preserved, show signs of the normal wear and tear inflicted through generations of use. It would be extremely atypical to find a piece in perfect condition, and one should approach with caution an antique that looks as if it just walked out of a cabinetmaker's shop. Chances are it just did, perhaps with a heavy dose of "aesthetic surgery."

While wear and tear is common to all objects, it doesn't happen in the exact same way for all pieces. In other words, depending on differing patterns of usage, a piece will show its age in one spot and not in another. Finishes show uneven wear due to differing degrees of sunlight to which the parts have been exposed, for example.

Fakers often forget these principles when they alter a work or compose a fake. An individual can use his or her hands to feel for the gentle rounding that softens sharp edges on tabletops or on arm supports. Some experts check to see if chairs pass the "shake test." Due to warping, shrinkage, and loosening of joints, most old chairs have a degree of movement or yield. Totally unyielding models should be suspicious to the touch. Rubbing sounds signal wear, where good wood is moving against wood. When a wear spot is tracked down, it should have a corresponding point of contact or friction. These are only several of the subtleties that affect a genuine antique—learning to recognize such qualities can significantly assist in determining authenticity of the article.

Repairs and Restorations ✒︎

oted American furniture dealer Albert Sack, of the firm Israel Sack, has outlined many of the following commonly occurring major restorations and repairs that afflict American antique furniture. The presence of any one may diminish the value of a piece. His book, *Fine Points of Furniture* (look for the expanded edition), with examples of "good," "better," and "best" is a bible for anyone wishing to improve his connoisseurship skills.

◆ **Addition of arms to what was once a side chair**
◆ **Reshaping of arms, wings, or crest rails (wing chairs)**
◆ **Reshaping of crest rail, arms, or seat frame into more desirable form (sofas)**

Case Pieces
◆ **Replacement of one or more legs**
◆ **Splicing, building up, or shortening of legs**
◆ **Enhancement through carving or reshaping to apron, drawers, or top**
◆ **Case reduction to accommodate smaller living space; change in shape from one form to another (for example, from flat to blocked)**
◆ **Marriages of old tops and bottoms, both pieces of which were originally part of another object**
◆ **Conversion of flat-top case to one with arched pediment**
◆ **Replacement or enhancement of original pediment**
◆ **Replacement of one or more doors or drawers**
◆ **Replacement of turned legs, stretchers, and feet**
◆ **Total replacement of veneered surface**
◆ **Re-inlay of large areas**
◆ **Replacement or embellishment of interiors**
◆ **Replacement of lids**
◆ **Replacement or addition of tambour doors**

Seating
◆ **Replacement of one or more legs**
◆ **Reshaping of seat frame into more desirable shape**
◆ **Replacement of stretchers**
◆ **Replacement of splat**
◆ **Replacement or alteration of crest rail**
◆ **Embellishment through carving to crest rail and/or legs**
◆ **Replacement of arm supports**

Courtesy Mabel Brady Garvan & C. Sanford Bull, BA 1893, collections (by Exchange) Yale University

Purportedly the product of the Pilgrim era, this chair is a complete fake. The turnings on the front legs are more indicative of William and Mary scale than heavyset Pilgrim scale. Its carved date, 1678, is a play on numbers, since this piece probably was made in 1867.

This mixing table is mixed up indeed. The base is actually the bottom half of a desk-on-frame. The marble mixing top is smaller than the base, which doesn't equate with period practice.

Tables

✦ **Replacement of feet, legs, stretchers, or drawers**
✦ **Reshaping of tops, leaves, or apron**
✦ **Replacement of stretchers or gates, tops, or leaves**
✦ **Reshaping of pedestal**
✦ **Enhancement of form through carving to pedestal or knee**
✦ **Replacement of top**
✦ **Re-veneering, re-turning, or a large amount of restoration to the frame**
✦ **Marriage of disparate top and pedestal or base**
✦ **Embellishment through inlay**

Bedsteads

✦ **Replacement of two vertical rails or two horizontal rails**
✦ **Replacement of headboard or footposts**
✦ **Scaling down**
✦ **Re-turning, re-reeding, or re-carving**

The presence of one of the major repairs or changes noted above would probably eliminate such a piece from the discerning collector's consideration. Those American antiques that are most coveted are those that are unsullied. Since this is virtually impossible, if only for reasons of the normal life expectancy of furniture, then those forms with honest repairs are acceptable.

What constitutes honest and acceptable repairs differs within the professional and collecting community, but certain repair standards are generally accepted. Honest repairs are considered those that are either meant to shore up a piece that would otherwise be lost, or are those that faithfully resurrect, from evidence or from similar example, features that have been damaged. The object is to assure the remaining integrity of the object, not to enhance or alter it to a more desirable form, as may be the case with frauds.

Experience dictates that most case furniture has lost its drawer pulls at some point during its lifespan. Replaced brasses are not at all uncommon and if the replacements are sensitively conceived with the original pulls in mind (perhaps from a remaining pull), they are acceptable. Absolute purists may be content with a case piece on which only several original pulls are present and no attempt has been made to reconstruct the lost ones. Common sense and patterns of usage also suggest that feet are susceptible parts on many forms. They can be ravaged by moisture, breakage, and by years of abuse inflicted by constant contact with the floor. Therefore, a careful and respectful replacement of one foot based on three remaining examples would be preferable to four replaced feet with no precedent. And it would be far more preferable to find deliberately new wood shoring up the bottom of a case piece or securing seats than to find totally replaced legs or seat frames.

These are only several suggestions as to what might constitute an honest repair. It takes practice and patience to understand the fine line an antique walks between being honestly repaired and being the subject of scurrilous alteration. Within the confines of the market, collectors must ultimately decide what is personally acceptable to them. Armed with some of the investigative techniques listed above, collectors will be able to make this decision more intelligently and with less consternation.

Happy Hunting!

SELECTED BIBLIOGRAPHY

Aronson, Joseph. *The Encyclopedia of Furniture.* 3rd ed. New York: Crown Publishers, Inc., 1965

Boorstin, Daniel J. *The Americans: The Colonial Experience.* New York: Random House, Inc., 1958

Chippendale, Thomas. *The Gentleman and Cabinet-Maker's Director.* 3rd ed. London: Privately printed, 1762. Reprint. New York: Dover Publications, 1966

Federico, Jean Taylor. *Clues to American Furniture.* Washington, D.C.: Starrhill Press, 1988

Forman, Benno M. *American Seating Furniture 1630–1730.* New York: W.W. Norton & Company, 1988

Davidson, Marshall B., and Stillinger, Elizabeth. *The American Wing at the Metropolitan Museum of Art.* New York: Harrison House, 1987

Davidson, Marshall B., ed., *Three Centuries of American Antiques.* Vol. I: *The American Heritage History of Colonial Antiques.* Vol. II: *The American Heritage History of American Antiques from the Revolution to the Civil War.* Vol. III: *The American Heritage History of Antiques from the Civil War to World War I.* Reprint (3 vol. in 1). New York: Bonanza Books, 1979

Fairbanks, Jonathan L., and Bates, Elizabeth Bidwell. *American Furniture 1620 to the Present.* New York: Richard Marek, 1981

Flanigan, J. Michael. *American Furniture from the Kaufman Collection.* Washington, D.C.: National Gallery of Art, 1986

Jobe, Brock, and Kaye, Myrna. *New England Furniture: The Colonial Era.* Boston: Houghton Mifflin Company, 1984

Hepplewhite, George. *The Cabinet-Maker and Upholsterer's Guide.* 3rd ed. London: I. & J. Taylor, 1984. Reprint. New York: Dover Publications, 1969

Kayne, Myrna. *Fake, Fraud, or Genuine?* Boston: Little, Brown, and Company, 1987

Montgomery, Charles F. *American Furniture: The Federal Period, in the Henry Francis duPont Winterthur Museum.* New York: Viking Press, 1966

Hayward, Helena, ed. *World Furniture.* London: The Hamlyn Publishing Group Limited, 1965

Kirk, John T. *American Chairs: Queen Anne and Chippendale.* New York: Alfred A. Knopf, 1972

_____. *American Furniture and the British Tradition to 1830.* New York: Alfred A. Knopf, 1982

_____. *Early American Furniture: How to Recognize, Evaluate, Buy and Care for the Most Beautiful Pieces—High-Style, Country, Primitive, and Rustic.* New York: Alfred A. Knopf, 1970

Sack, Albert. *Fine Points of Furniture Early American.* New York: Crown Publishers, Inc., 1950

Sheraton, Thomas. *The Cabinet-Maker and Upholsterer's Drawing-Book.* 3rd rev. ed. London: T. Bensley, 1802. Reprint. Charles F. Montgomery and Wilfred P. Cole, eds. New York: Praeger Publishers, 1970

Ward, Gerald W. R., and Hosley, William N., Jr. *The Great River Art & Society of the Connecticut Valley, 1635–1820.* Hartford: Wadsworth Atheneum, 1985

Watson, Sir Francis, introduction by. *The History of Furniture.* New York: Crescent Books, 1982

Weidman, Gregory R. *Furniture in Maryland 1740–1940.* Baltimore: Maryland Historical Society, 1984

APPENDIX: VIEWING AMERICAN ANTIQUE FURNITURE

One of the best ways to enhance connoisseurship in the field of American antique furniture is to view as many period pieces as possible. Listed below are some of the many institutions and museums where American furniture can be found.

Albany Institute of History and Art, Albany, New York
Art Institute of Chicago, Chicago, Illinois
Baltimore Museum of Art, Baltimore, Maryland
Brooklyn Museum, Brooklyn, New York
Cincinnati Art Museum, Cincinnati , Ohio
Colonial Williamsburg, Williamsburg, Virginia
Concord Antiquarian Museum, Concord, Massachusetts
Connecticut Historical Society, Hartford, Connecticut
Daughters of the American Revolution Museum, Washington, D.C.
Diplomatic Reception Rooms, U.S. Department of State, Washington, D.C.
Essex Institute, Salem, Massachusetts
Henry Ford Museum and Greenfield Village, Dearborn, Michigan
Henry Francis duPont Winterthur Museum, Winterthur, Delaware
High Museum of Art, Atlanta, Georgia
Historic Charleston Foundation, Charleston, South Carolina
Historic Deerfield, Deerfield, Massachusetts
Maryland Historical Society, Baltimore, Maryland
Metropolitan Museum of Art, American Wing, New York, New York
Monmouth County Historical Association, Freehold, New Jersey
Museum of Early Southern Decorative Arts, Winston-Salem, North Carolina
Museum of Fine Arts, Boston, Massachusetts
Museum of Fine Arts, Bayou Bend Collection, Houston, Texas
New Haven Colony Historical Society, New Haven, Connecticut
Newport Historical Society, Newport, Rhode Island
New York Historical Society, New York, New York
Old Sturbridge Village, Sturbridge, Massachusetts
Peter Foulger Museum, Nantucket Historical Association, Nantucket, Massachusetts
Philadelphia Museum of Art, Philadelphia, Pennsylvania
Pilgrim Hall, Plymouth, Massachusetts
Rhode Island Historical Society, Providence, Rhode Island
Rhode Island School of Design, Museum of Art, Providence, Rhode Island
Society for the Preservation of New England Antiquities, Boston and New England
Strawberry Banke, Portsmouth, New Hampshire
Wadsworth Atheneum, Hartford, Connecticut
Yale University Art Gallery, Mabel Brady Garvan and Related Collections, New Haven, Connecticut

STYLE IDENTIFIERS

Following are some general traits that can help pinpoint specific period styles.

PILGRIM FURNITURE

Fig. 1 A mortise-and-tenon joint, the primary joinery technique of Pilgrim era furniture. **Fig. 2** Hand-forged rose-headed nails used in furniture construction up to about 1790. **Fig. 3** Seventeenth-century split spindle. Formed when two blocks of wood were glued together separated only by a thin strip of wood. After turning to desired shape, the thin strip of wood was knocked out, creating two halves or "splits" that were applied to case pieces. **Fig. 4** Carved panel of sunflower and tulip. Highly stylized ornament found on Wethersfield chests.

WILLIAM AND MARY FURNITURE

Fig. 5 Ball foot commonly found on William and Mary case pieces. **Fig. 6** Example of dovetail construction on drawer side, a cabinet-making technique first used during the William and Mary period. **Fig. 7** Teardrop drawer pull. **Fig. 8** (l) Baluster-and-cup turned leg often found on New York furniture; (r) cup-and-trumpet turned leg.

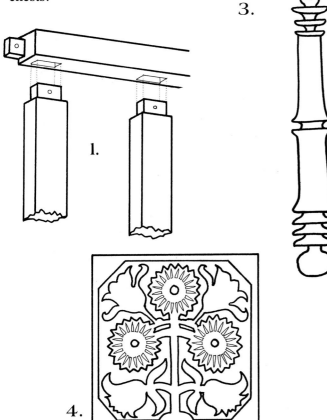

1.

2.

3.

4.

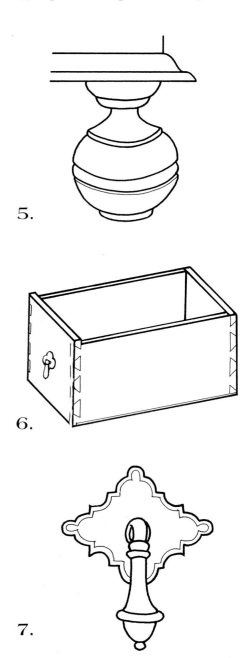

5.

6.

7.

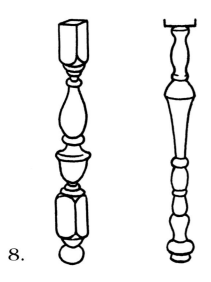

8.

QUEEN ANNE FURNITURE

Fig. 9 Cabriole leg ending in pad foot. **Fig. 10** Trifid foot, especially popular on Philadelphia chairs. **Fig. 11** Rounded crest rail with carved shell. **Fig. 12** Stylized inlaid star characteristic of Boston Queen Anne pieces.

CHIPPENDALE FURNITURE

Fig. 13 Cabriole leg ending in claw-and-ball foot with heavy foliate carving at the knee. **Fig. 14** Straight leg with stop-fluted leg, especially popular in Newport. **Fig. 15** Marlborough leg with blocked foot and knee bracket found frequently in Philadelphia. **Fig. 16** Ogee bracket foot used exclusively on case furniture. **Fig. 17** Chippendale-style flattened urn brass with bail pull. **Fig. 18** Curvilinear foliate ornament with asymmetrical composition.

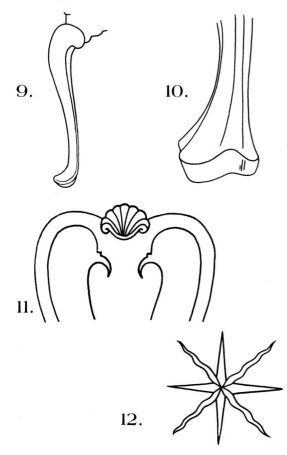

9.   10.

11.

12.

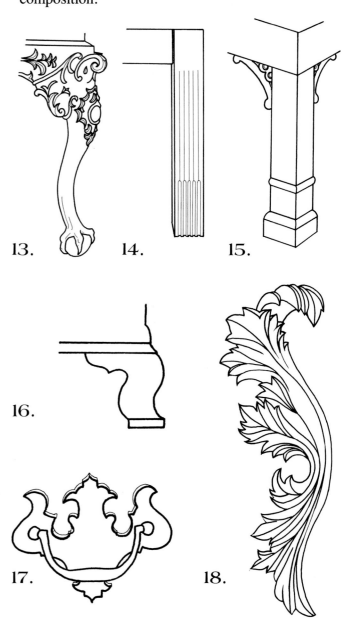

13.   14.   15.

16.

17.   18.

FEDERAL FURNITURE

Fig. 19 Delicately proportioned shield-back side chair with incurved rear legs and front spade feet. **Fig. 20** Stringing, or thin inlay of contrasting woods, used as accent on straight surfaces.
Fig. 21 Patera and bellflower inlay, two of the most popular Federal patterns. **Fig. 22** Tapered leg ending in spade foot reminiscent of Hepplewhite designs.

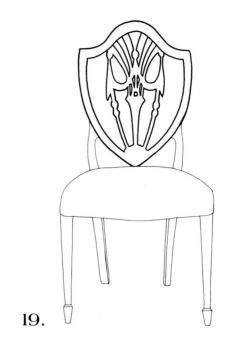

19.

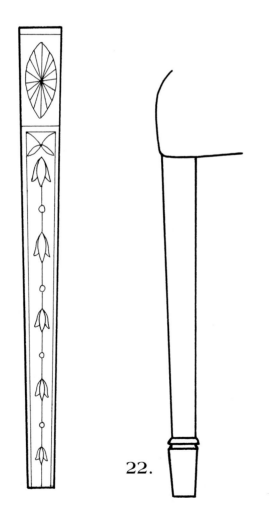

20.

21.   22.

EMPIRE FURNITURE

Fig. 23 Klismos chair with integrated curved back and splayed legs based on chair from antiquity.
Fig. 24 Lyre motif used on various Empire forms. **Fig. 25** Section of Empire sofa with scrolled arm, acanthus-leaf carving, cornucopia bracket, and heavy animal paw foot. **Fig. 26** Lion's head with brass ring pull.

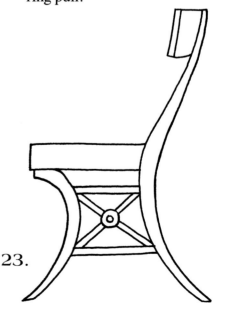

23.

24.

Fig. 27 C-scroll foot, a common component of the period.
Fig. 28 S-scroll support, square in section. **Fig. 29** Glass drawer pull.

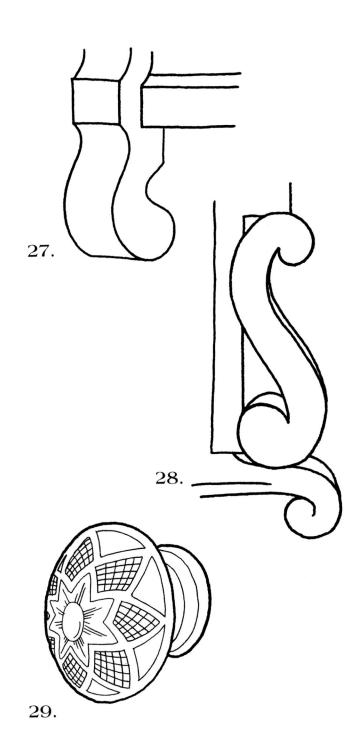

27.

28.

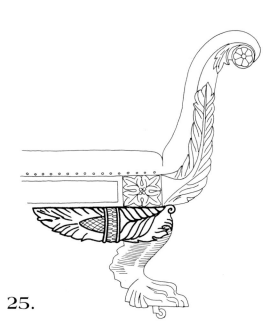

25.

26.

29.

CHIPPENDALE CHAIR

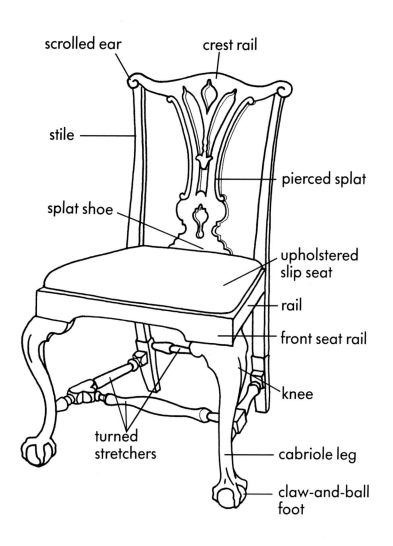

scrolled ear

crest rail

stile

splat shoe

pierced splat

upholstered slip seat

rail

front seat rail

knee

turned stretchers

cabriole leg

claw-and-ball foot

WILLIAM AND MARY CHAIR

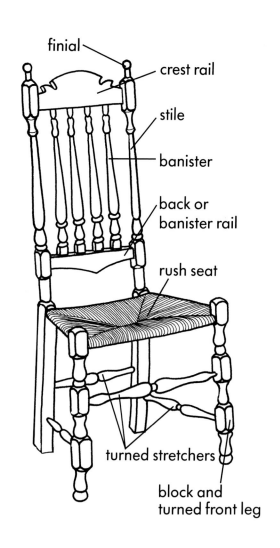

finial

crest rail

stile

banister

back or banister rail

rush seat

turned stretchers

block and turned front leg

WILLIAM AND MARY GATE-LEG TABLE

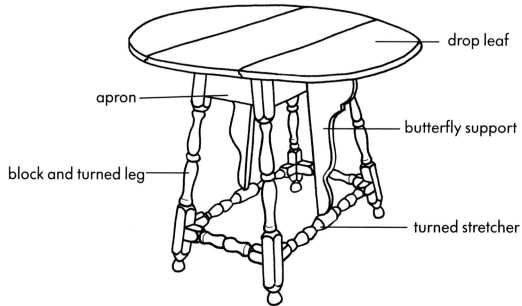

drop leaf

apron

butterfly support

block and turned leg

turned stretcher

QUEEN ANNE HIGH CHEST

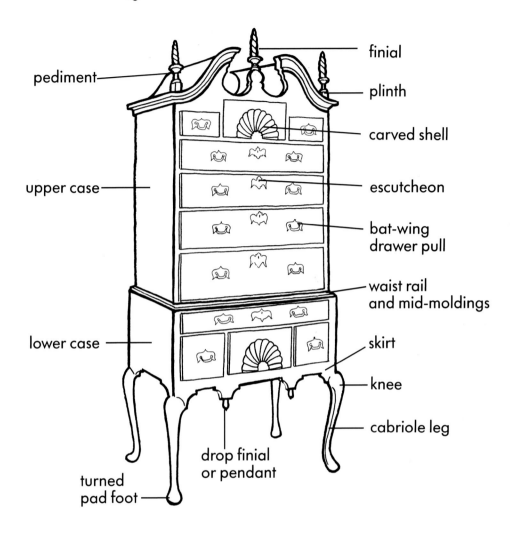

pediment

finial

plinth

carved shell

upper case

escutcheon

bat-wing
drawer pull

waist rail
and mid-moldings

lower case

skirt

knee

cabriole leg

drop finial
or pendant

turned
pad foot

FEDERAL SOFA

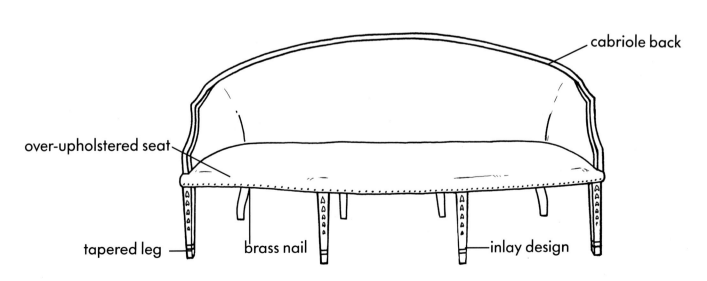

cabriole back

over-upholstered seat

tapered leg

brass nail

inlay design

GLOSSARY

Acanthus. A decorative ornament based on the leaves of the acanthus plant. Used in classical times, it became very popular in the eighteenth and nineteenth centuries.

Apron. The horizontal piece of wood below a case piece, seat, or tabletop—sometimes referred to as a skirt.

Baluster. An upright support or turned vertical post, often resembling a vase or column. Also called a banister.

Banister-back chair. A chair back made of turned upright banisters or balusters that are usually topped by a crest rail and supported by a lower cross rail above the seat. It was popular in the eighteenth century.

Baroque. European seventeenth-century design that stressed brilliant and exaggerated forms. It influenced the William and Mary and Queen Anne styles.

Bat wing. The drawer hardware that resembled a bat's wing, the shape was a popular choice for case furniture of the eighteenth century.

Bedstead. The hard-good component or frame, which today is called a bed.

Bird-cage. A supporting section of a tilt-top table made up of two blocks with columns between the top and base that allows the table to tilt and pivot.

Block-front. On case pieces, a front that is divided into three vertical sections; the center is concave and the two flanking sections are convex. It was especially popular in the eighteenth century in Newport and Boston.

Bombé. Also called a kettle base, case pieces of this shape have bases that are rounded with bulging sides. It was found on Chippendale furniture made in the Boston area.

Bonnet top. A pediment that forms a hood or top to a case piece. Popular in colonial furniture of the Queen Anne and Chippendale periods.

Boss. A raised, applied ornament of oval or round shape found on Pilgrim-era furniture such as chests and cupboards. Also called a jewel.

Boston chair. A period term of the early eighteenth century used to describe a leather-upholstered chair that was the linchpin of Boston's furniture trade. It was shipped throughout the colonies.

Boullework. Credited to André-Charles Boulle, this process was the Baroque technique of inlay that introduced wood or exotic materials to embellish surface. It was revived in some Empire designs, especially with brass.

Brewster chair. A turned chair of the Pilgrim era with spindles in the chair back and below the seat and arms. It was named for a chair owned by Elder William Brewster of Massachusetts.

Bun foot. A turned foot that is slightly compressed on top and bottom. It was popular on late Pilgrim and William and Mary pieces.

Bureau-table. A chest of drawers with a recessed area in the center for the sitter's legs. Also called a kneehole desk, the form was made during the Chippendale period.

Butterfly table. A descriptive term for the winged brackets that support the large leaves on a small drop-leaf table. The form was favored in the William and Mary period, especially in Connecticut.

Cabriole leg. A curved leg with an outcurved knee and an incurved ankle, it has the shape of an inverted S-curve. Usually terminating in a pad or claw-and-ball foot, it often appeared on Queen Anne and Chippendale furniture.

Campeachy chair. A slung seat over a curule base that was derived from ancient models. It was popularized in the nineteenth century by Thomas Jefferson.

Carver chair. Named for a chair owned by Governor John Carver, this turned Pilgrim-era chair has spindles only on the back.

Case furniture. Based on the box shape, case pieces are used for storage.

Chest-on-chest. A case piece made of two separate chests that are placed on top of each other and meant to function as one object.

Chinoiserie. Western interpretation of Oriental motifs. The style was popular in the William and Mary, Queen Anne, and Chippendale periods.

Chippendale. A popular style in America from the mid-eighteenth century until the Revolution, it incorporated elements from the Rococo or modern French, Gothic, and Chinese novelties. Irregular and naturalistic forms predominate.

Claw-and-ball foot. A carved foot that depicts a claw grasping a ball, it was the terminus for many cabriole legs. The shape was subject to regional interpretations in colonial America.

Club foot. A thick, slightly pointed foot with a more aggressive curve than that of the pad foot, it has a defined edge above the shoe.

Commode. A low chest of drawers or cabinet based on a popular French form not often found in American cabinetmaking.

Compass seat. Also known as a horseshoe seat, the term was coined from the flared outline of a compass.

Corner chair. A chair with one leg in front, one in the rear, and one at each side. Also called a roundabout chair, it was frequently paired with a desk.

Cornice. Horizontal molding that usually projects from the top of the case piece to which it is attached.

Cornucopia. A horn-shaped container filled with flowers and/or fruit. It was a common horizontally affixed motif on early to mid-nineteenth-century furniture.

Crest rail. The horizontal top rail of a chair of sofa. The shape was dependent on the period involved but many were elaborately carved.

Cromwellian chair. Also called a farthingale chair, an armless square form resembling a stool with an upholstered back. It was popular in the seventeenth century.

Cupboard. A status piece of case furniture in Pilgrim era. Models with an enclosed storage space above and an open shelf below are called court cupboards while models with upper and lower enclosed storage areas are called press cupboards.

Curule. Curules or magistrates in ancient Rome used pieces with X-shaped bases and curved legs. The shape re-emerged in nineteenth-century Empire designs.

Daybed. A multi-legged, armless lounge chair introduced during the William and Mary period. Also called a couch, it was usually upholstered or covered with cane or rush.

Dentil molding. Decorative trim in the shape of small rectangles separate with gaps that resemble a row of teeth.

Dovetail. Formed from interlocking, flared tenons that resemble a dove's tail, this technique ushered in the era of cabinetmaking starting in the William and Mary period.

Ears. The projections on Chippendale period chairs that curve out from the top of the crest rail.

Easy chair. A wing chair. Used primarily by the elderly and ill, this padded and upholstered chair first appeared in the William and Mary period and was used in the bed chamber.

Églomisé. Decorative reverse painting or gilding on glass. It was a popular ornamentation on early Neoclassical furniture, especially in Baltimore.

Elbow chair. Period terminology for an armchair.

Empire. The second expression of Neoclassicism characterized by a growing concern for archaeological accuracy in furniture design from 1815 to 1840. French Empire and English Regency styles were converging influences.

Fancy furniture. Furniture painted with polychrome paint depicting floral motifs or scenery. It was found frequently on Baltimore furniture of the Empire period.

Fat classical. Furniture of the late Empire period that is characterized by swollen forms of classical shape.

Federal. The first stage of Neoclassicism in America beginning in the early nineteenth century and coinciding with the formation of the federal government. The forms are predominately geometric and fine of scale.

Field bedstead. A bedstead with a canopy based on models used by the military.

Finial. A carved or turned decorative ornament of various shapes that is used as a crown on pediments. A pendant finial drops downward and is usually found on the apron or skirt of case pieces.

Flemish scroll. The primary decorative device of the William and Mary period. Found mostly on chairs, it was made up of carved C-shaped and S-scrolls.

Fluting. Parallel horizontal concave channels used as a decorative device.

Fretwork. Decorative trim of open-cut patterns formed by the fret saw or carved. Found mostly on tops and sides of case pieces, especially in the Chippendale period.

Gate-leg table. A drop-leaf table on which the legs are connected by stretchers. The legs act as swinging gates and extend to support the top. Models without stretchers are called swing-leg tables.

Gondola chair. A chair of the Restauration period with an open back and a wide, solid back splat. The upright stiles that form the back curve around and act as supports for the arms.

Gothic. A novelty of the Chippendale style drawing on several periods of English architecture and incorporating portions of the skeleton framework in forms. These novelties included pointed arches and foils, often mixed with Chinese and Rococo elements.

Grisaille. Monochromatic tones of gray paint used on the Dutch kas to simulate the floral carvings of expensive European models.

Hadley chest. Named for the Hadley area of Massachusetts in the Upper Connecticut River Valley, a Pilgrim-era chest with drawers of joined construction and three panels on the front, which was carved with meandering floral motifs.

High chest. A case piece with two sections, the lower portion standing on legs. The status object in eighteenth-century households, its modern name is a highboy.

Huntboard. A long, high table of shallow depth that was preferred over the sideboard in some Southern locales. Originally a board or frame from which to serve drinks after the fox hunt. When combined with drawers or cabinets, it is called a hunt sideboard.

Inlay. A decorative treatment set into the surface that uses wood or other materials to form texture or bands of color (stringing), pictorial images (marquetry), or geometric shapes (parquetry).

Jacobean. Related to the reign of King James I (1603–1625) in England, the term is sometimes used to describe American furniture of the Pilgrim era.

Japanning. The western practice of imitating Oriental lacquerwork. A wood base was covered with paint, and motifs were built up with gesso and gilded or silvered. It was a somewhat fragile but popular technique in the early to mid-eighteenth century, especially in Boston.

Joinery. The seventeenth-century practice of constructing objects based on the mortise-and-tenon joint. A tenon, or tongue, was fitted into a mortise, or hole, at right angles that were secured by a peg or pin.

Kas. A large wardrobe or press with heavy raised and carved panels or painted surfaces. Made by settlers from the Low Countries, the form appealed to the Dutch settlers of the New York area.

Klismos. A side chair first designed by the ancient Greeks with a concave-curved back and splayed legs. The form was the prototype for much Empire seating design.

Lolling chair. An armchair of the Federal period with a high-upholstered back and seat and exposed arms, the form was a specialty of New England chairmakers. Also called a Martha Washington chair.

Lowboy. A modern term for a low case piece on legs that was often made en suite with a high chest.

Lyre. A stringed instrument from classical antiquity that was popular on Neoclassical pieces, especially in New York.

Marlborough leg. A straight, square leg, sometimes ending in a blocked foot prevalent on Chippendale forms.

Méridienne. A sofa of asymmetrical form based on French examples with one arm lower than the other.

Monopodium. An animal foot and head in a single arrangement based on ancient models. Found most often on case pieces of the Empire era.

Mortise and tenon. A system of seventeenth-century joinery that fitted a tenon, or tongue, from one piece of wood into a mortise, or hole, on another piece, the joint of which was secured by a peg.

Neoclassicism. A nineteenth-century trend in furniture design that looked to antiquity for inspiration. It progressed through three stages in America—Federal, Empire, and Restauration.

Ogee. An S-shaped molding. Also known as a cyma curve.

Ormolu. Bronze decorative mounts covered in gilt that appeared in abundance in the Empire period, especially in the work of French-trained Charles-Honoré Lannuier.

Oxbow front. Also known as a reverse serpentine curve, the oxbow moves first out, then in, then out across a surface. It was popular in Chippendale case pieces.

Pad foot. A gently rounded or oval foot found on Queen Anne legs and Chippendale legs as an alternative to costly claw-and-ball feet.

Paintbrush foot. Found on William and Mary chairs, the shape resembles the bristles of a paintbrush. Also dubbed a Spanish foot, although the true origin of the foot is Portuguese.

Patina. The result of years of wax, dirt, and oxidation, it is the texture and color in the finish of antique objects.

Pattern book. Renderings of period pieces designed for cabinetmakers that helped disseminate specific styles beginning in the Queen Anne period and continuing to the present.

Paw foot. Carved to represent an animal's paw, it was used infrequently on very high-style Chippendale pieces. It reappeared in swollen form during the Empire period, the fattest forms of which are termed "fat classical."

Pedestal table. A table with a columnar base derived from those found at the ancient digs of Rome. It was popular in Neoclassical design.

Pediment. On chests and secretaries, the crowning top that replicates architectural projections on classical buildings. It can be arched or triangular.

Pembroke table. A variant of the drop-leaf table usually with four square legs and drop leaves that are wider than the center section. Sometimes called a breakfast table, it was popular in the Chippendale and Federal periods.

Piecrust table. A tripod table with a circular top and scalloped edges in the shape of a piecrust. These tables were often identified as tea tables in the eighteenth century.

Pier table. A table originally built to stand against a pier or the wall between two windows. The form reached its height of popularity in the nineteenth century.

Pilgrim. The seventeenth-century design centering on sturdy rectilinear forms, mortise-and-tenon construction, and turned and carved members. It was influenced by medieval furniture as well as by Renaissance-inspired forms of Anglo-Flemish origin.

Pillar and Scroll. The last stage of Neoclassicism in nineteenth-century furniture characterized by simple square-section shapes in the form of pillars and scrolls.

Prince of Wales feathers. A carved ornamental motif of three ostrich feathers, the symbol of the Prince of Wales. It was used in Federal period chairs, especially high-style versions found in Salem and New York.

Queen Anne. Late Baroque colonial-style furniture dating from 1725 to 1755. It was characterized by the S-curve and an architectural underpinning that typified many pieces.

Rail. A horizontal piece of wood that joins vertical members.

Reeding. Repetitive vertical carved convex ornaments.

Restauration. A simplified version of the French Empire style that favored broad plain veneers and simple scrolled shapes cut from band saws. Also known as the Pillar and Scroll style, it marked the last stage of Neoclassicism from 1830 to 1840.

Ribbon-back splat. A splat that resembles gathered ribbons worked into the back. Based on designs from Chippendale's *Director,* the form was found on the highest-style chairs.

Rococo. Originating in eighteenth-century France, it was the "modern French taste," one component of the Chippendale style in England and America. It was composed of lively free-form organic ornament and curvilinear forms.

Rose-headed nails. Hand-forged nails made during the eighteenth century. The name derives from the rose shape of the hammered nails.

Saber leg. Derived from the Greek klismos, the saber leg curves inward to form a graceful S-shaped profile.

Scroll-back chair. A period term for the Greek klismos.

Scroll foot. A chair foot shaped like a rolled-up scroll that was found on high-style Chippendale chairs as an alternative to the claw-and-ball foot. Also known as a whorl foot, it was used alternately to describe the William and Mary Spanish or paintbrush foot.

Serpentine. Opposite of the oxbow curve, it moves in, out, and in across the surface. It was a popular treatment on Chippendale case pieces.

Settee. A small sofa with arms and a back.

Settle. A wooden bench with a high back and arms formed from boards often used in front of fireplaces and as an informal room divider. Primarily an object of the Pilgrim era, with later revivals.

Shield-back chair. A chair with a shield commonly found in the Federal style. Called a "vase-back" if the shield was pointed and an "urn-back" if the shield was rounded. Other popular shapes were the oval-back and the heart-back.

Sideboard. A low and wide chest of drawers or compartments on legs. Used against a wall or in an alcove of the dining room beginning in the Federal period to display and serve food.